A

DESCRIPTION

OF THE

ROADS

IN

BENGAL AND BAHAR

A DESCRIPTION OF THE ROADS IN BENGAL AND BAHAR

JAMES RENNELL

Published by

Gyan Publishing House
5, Ansari Road
Daryaganj, New Delhi-110002
Phone: 011-47034999, 9811692060
E-mail: books@gyanbooks.com

Distribution Network
gyanbooks.com
India, USA, Canada, UK, Australia

ISBN: 978-93-7169-252-6 (PB)

First Published, 1779

2nd Impression 2025

Printed at: Gyan Press, Delhi.

A DESCRIPTION OF THE ROADS IN BENGAL AND BAHAR
Author: JAMES RENNELL

A DESCRIPTION OF THE ROADS IN BENGAL AND BAHAR.

CONTAINING

I. The direct Roads from CALCUTTA to all the Cities, Towns, and Places of Note in Bengal and Bahar; shewing the measured Distances between the Stages, and the Number and Situation of the Fords and Ferries that are to be crossed.

II. III. IV. The direct Roads from the Three other principal Cities, viz. MOORSHEDABAD, PATNA, and DACCA; arranged in the same Manner.

V. The Cross Roads from the subordinate Military Stations and Factories, to all the Places of Note within their respective Neighbourhoods: With an Index.

BY JAMES RENNELL,

Late Major of Engineers and Surveyor General to the Honourable the East India Company.

Printed by order of the Honourable the COURT of DIRECTORS of the said Company. 1778.

PREFACE.

THE honourable the COURT OF DIRECTORS having thought proper to print the BOOK OF ROADS IN BENGAL AND BAHAR for the uſe of the *Company's Servants* in thoſe provinces, I have added to it as much as I thought was wanting to render it a complete travelling guide, as far as relates to diſtances, and the nature of the rivers that interſect the roads. The utility of ſuch a work in *any* country muſt ſtrike every one: much more in a country where the people employed by Government are mere ſojourners, and from the want of local knowledge muſt depend upon the information of Guides, who often miſlead them either through ignorance or intereſted motives. At beſt, thoſe guides know only the moſt frequented roads; ſo that in croſſing the country no information whatever can be derived from them: and as for the peaſantry, or *ryots*, they cannot be ſuppoſed to know the roads beyond the circle of the markets which they frequent.

As the mode of arrangement here differs from that of all other Books of Roads that I have ſeen, I may be expected to ſet forth my reaſon for adopting it, which is, that I conſider CALCUTTA, MOORSHEDABAD, PATNA, and DACCA, as the places where theſe Tables will be in the moſt general uſe (the firſt being the ſeat of government, and the others either the capital military ſtations, or factories, or both) and therefore I have framed a ſeparate Table or ſet of Tables for each, for the eaſe and convenience of the people reſiding there: ſo that, in fact, theſe four cities may be conſidered as *centres* from whence all the great roads iſſue. The articles in each ſet are alphabetically arranged, to prevent the neceſſity of having a number of Indexes.

The

The Table for CALCUTTA does not refer to any of the others; and may therefore form a ſeparate book, as well as a part of the general work. The other three Tables for MOORSHEDABAD, PATNA, and DACCA, are, by a mutual reference to each other, and to the CALCUTTA Table, equally complete with the firſt, but cannot be ſeparated. A Fifth Table contains the *principal* CROSS ROADS; with an INDEX pointing out the roads from about twenty-eight ſtations in different parts of the provinces to every place of note within their reſpective neighbourhoods. Theſe ſtations are either the ſeats of provincial councils, or of collectors; ſubordinate military ſtations, or factories; or places, which from their ſituation are likely to become military poſts in time of invaſion. It is expected that this latter part of the work will be highly uſeful to Officers who command detachments on actual ſervice, as my own experience has repeatedly convinced me how much it is wanted.

A ſmall Map, which is to be bound up with it, will render the book ſtill more complete, by combining the idea of the reſpective poſitions of places with that of the diſtances.

As there is ſcarce a place of note within the provinces omitted in the four Tables, a traveller cannot be at a loſs to find his route to either of the four cities: for if he ſhould be off the great road, he cannot be many miles from ſome one place mentioned in the Tables. And the Index to the Croſs Roads being equally copious, the roads to the provincial towns will be found as eaſily.

So great a number of references as occur in the book may by ſome be thought troubleſome, or perhaps unneceſſary; but every diſcerning perſon will be convinced that an equal number of repetitions would have ſwelled the book beyond the ſize of a pocket volume, and totally deſtroyed the intention of printing it.

Obſerve

Obſerve in the Tables, that when a reference is made to a *place*, without mentioning the *page*, it means a place in the *ſame* table from whence the reference is made. On the contrary, when the *page* is mentioned, it refers to ſome *other* Table. For an inſtance of the firſt kind---Look at *Ambooah* in the table for CALCUTTA, which ſtands as follows: [Ambooah. See Patna, 1ſt road, 49 . 0.] Here it means that you are to look for the particulars of the road to *Ambooah* under the article PATNA in the *ſame* Table; and that the whole diſtance is 49 miles. For an inſtance of the ſecond kind---Look at *Bettyah* in the Table for MOORSHEDABAD. You are firſt referred to PATNA (page 55) where the portion of road between MOORSHEDABAD and PATNA is included in the road from CALCUTTA to PATNA. And next to *Bettyah* (page 10) for the road from PATNA to *Bettyah*: the road from MOORSHEDABAD to *Bettyah* leading through PATNA.

The references in the Index to the CROSS ROADS are rather more troubleſome, by reaſon that the order of the lines muſt ſometimes be reverſed: as for inſtance, in the road from *Dinagepour* to MAULDAH (page 156). Here, in reverſing the diſtances, care muſt be taken not to miſplace them: for one might be apt to read 6 . 2 inſtead of 8 . 6 for the diſtance between *Dinagepour* and *Futtypour*.

Although no more than about 28 ſtations will be found in the Index, yet by attending to the alphabetical liſts under each ſtation, many more routes may be found. For inſtance, although *Deogur* is not choſen as a ſtation, yet as the roads from moſt of the weſtern ſtations to that place are inſerted, it is evident that by reverſing them, the ſame purpoſe is anſwered as if *Deogur* had been made a ſtation. The ſame of many other places. A very little practice will make the uſe of the Index familiar; and its advantages, I have no doubt, will overbalance the trouble of turning over the book.

With

With respect to the *Rivers*---It is well known to Gentlemen who have resided in BENGAL, that few rivers or nullahs that exist in the dry season, can be fordable during the rainy season, or for some months afterwards: *the fords therefore must be understood to continue only from December to June.*

The Distances, which are in *Statute* Miles and Furlongs, are reckoned from the following Standards:

In Calcutta	- -	from *Old Fort William.*
Moorshedabad		from *the Palace of Mootyjyl.*
Patna	- -	from *the Kellah.*
Dacca	- -	from *the English Factory.*
Burdwan	- -	from *the English Factory.*
Dinagepour	-	from *Rajegunge Bazar.*
Islamabad	- -	from *the Old Fort.*

And from the *centres* of all the other stations.

The *Coss* of HINDOSTAN is about two *Statute* Miles and a sixteenth; as appears by the measurement of the Road from MOORSHEDABAD to PATNA taken by order of the Emperor. But the *computed Coss* of BENGAL and BAHAR is commonly less than two miles, and varies more than a fourth part in different quarters of the Provinces. By comparing the distances in the Tables with the horizontal distances in the Map, it will be found that one mile in seven is taken up by the windings of the Roads; which, considering the flatness and openness of the country, is a circumstance that one would not expect.

As most parts of BENGAL and BAHAR are level, or nearly so, the Sun's rising and setting may, in clear weather, be as easily discerned as at sea; I have therefore added a Table of the time of the Sun's rising and setting, as it furnishes the easiest method of regulating time for common purposes.

CONTENTS.

E R R A T A.

Page 14. article Buggura—for *Taïtah*, read *Taltah*.
Page 24. art. Dacca 2d road—after **Churan, omit** *Nullah*.
Page 24. after Tagoorpour, read *Nullah*.
Page 26. laſt line—for 344 . 4. read 347.
Page 28. for *Curallyah*, read *Curattyah*.
Page 55. for *Furruckaband*, read *Furruckabad*.
Page 98. for *Cutſee*, read *Cuſtee*.
Page 103. line 2d—for *Pecculoe*, read ***Pucculoe***.
Page 110. article Jungipour—after Churka, **read** *Coſſimbazar River—ferry*.
Page 181. for *Munſtangur*, read *Muſtangur*.
Page 190. for *Eeteneah*, read *Eetnah*.
Page 196. for *Santgutchy*, read *Sautgutchy*.
Page 233. for *Dulſingerra*, read *Dulſingjerra*.
Page 249. for *Tamoicla*, read *Tamoila*.

TABLES OF ROADS,

FROM

CALCUTTA,

TO ALL THE

PRINCIPAL PLACES

IN

BENGAL AND BAHAR.

EXPRESSING THE

DISTANCES BETWEEN THE STAGES, AND THE NUMBER AND SITUATION OF THE FORDS AND FERRIES THAT ARE TO BE CROSSED.

LONDON:
PRINTED IN THE YEAR MDCCLXXVIII.

TABLES OF ROADS,

From CALCUTTA, to all the principal Places in BENGAL and BAHAR.

N. B. The Articles marked thus *, are either inferred from the Maps, or taken from Sketches and Journals of Travellers; and thoſe in the following Characters, viz.

PATNA	are	Cities.
PURNEAH		Capitals of Provinces.
Nautpour		Towns and Places of Note.

Names of Places.	diſtances in Miles	and Furl.	Rivers and Nullahs to be croſſed.	ford or ferry
AHMIRABADS Purgunnah - - -				
Chandergunge, in Iſlamabad road - - -	234	4		
Buzra Cutcherry -	6	2		
	240	6		
AMBOOAH				
See PATNA, 1ſt road -	49	0		
AMMERPOUR				
PURNEAH - -	263	3		
Mulcowl - -	9	4		
Baſſatra - -	8	2		
Pachera - - -	7	5		
Saibgunge - -	6	4		
Nautpour - -	13	4	Coſa R.	fer.
Pattry - - -	6	6		
Joppa Burarya -	8	6		
AMMERPOUR -	15	0		
	339	2		

Names of Places.	distances in Miles and Furl.		Rivers and Nullahs to be crossed.	ford or ferry
ARRAH. See BENARES 1st road - - -	438	2		
ATTYAH. See Susung.	183	4		
AUGURDEEP. See PATNA 1st road - - -	78	3		
AWMORE Purgunnah				
Nulhatty in Patchwarry road	139	6		
Kanpour - - -	6	7		
Noangong - - -	9	2	Bansli R.	ford
Puccoree Cutcherry -	10	4		
	166	3		
AYTURAH. See PATNA 3d road - -	139	5		
AZMERIGUNGE				
Cutchua haut in Silhet road	249	4		
Lacki - - -	11	0	Kohi N.	ford
Beetalung - -	12	6	Brack R.	fer.
Azmerigunge - -	8	2		
	281	4		
BACKERGUNGE. 1st road by Jessore Culna				
Mullickpour, in DACCA road - -	36	0		
Sooty - - -	6	3	Jubuna N.	ford
Chandurya - -	6	1	Issamot R.	fer.
Bidaboxa - - -	6	6	Nullah	fer.
Mirjanagur - -	9	1	Cobbaduck R.	fer.
	64	3		

Names of Places.	distances in Miles	and Furl.	Rivers and Nullahs to be crossed.	ford or ferry.
Backergunge continued)	64	3		
Ramnagur - -	7	4		
Eckterpour - - -	11	5	Nullah	fer.
Samgunge - -	8	6		
Collispour - -	6	0		
Culna - - - -	2	4	Boirub R.	fer.
Jerryah - - -	10	6		
Rynabad - -	4	2	Nullah	fer.
Haholly - - -	6	3	Nullah	fer.
Molgam - - -	11	0	Ballisore R.	fer.
Iraun - - -	8	7	3 Nullahs	fers.
Sutalury - - -	8	5	2 ditto	fers.
Backergunge - -	11	3	2 ditto	fers.
	162	0		
BACKERGUNGE, 2d road, by Hobibgunge [the best]				
MOORLEY, in DACCA road	74	1		
Daudpour - - -	6	4	Boirub	fer.
Samrool - - -	9	0		
Mayescola - - -	5	0	Sittarya	fer.
Kolna - - - -	11	0	Nowgonga	fer.
Coyra - - -	6	0	Mudamutty	fer.
Muxoodpour -	7	6		
Batcamara - -	8	4		
Dignagur - - -	4	6		
Hobibgunge - - -	11	0	Comar	ford.
Kalkenny - - -	9	6	ditto	ford.
Gurnaddy - -	12	0		
Idracpour - -	5	6	Creek	fer.
Madapassa - -	12	6	3 Nullahs	fers.
Gorypassa - -	8	6	3 ditto	fers.
Backergunge -	7	4	Nullah	fer.
	200	1		
BAHAR 1st road. See PATNA 2d road 2d road. See PATNA 3d ditto	297	1		

Names of Places.	diſtances in Miles	and Furl.	Rivers and Nullahs to be croſſed.	ford or ferry.
BAHAR 3d road, by Monghir				
Rampour, in PATNA 1ſt road - - -	326	1		
Balguda - - -	5	2	2 Nullahs	fors.
Maſſora - - -	9	2		
Sheikpour - -	6	4		
Cooſera - -	7	4		
Palany - - -	6	6	Sacry N.	ford
BAHAR - -	8	6		
	370	1		
BALLASORE. See Ganjam	141	0		
BALLITUNGY				
Augurdeep, in Patna 1ſt road	78	3		
Pangotta - -	8	4	Nullah	fer.
Ballitunghy - -	11	6		
	98	5		
BAMINY				
Molgan, in Backergunge 1ſt road - -	133	1		
Sujagunge -	3	2	Damorda R.	fer.
* Charcolly	13	4		
* *Baminy* - - -	13	0		
	162	7		
BANGAH, in Silhet				
Sunerampour, in Silhet road	235	6		
Calligoſs - -	6	4		
Hurringber -	10	7	Bemalya	ford.
Chandpour - -	11	1		
Rajoorah - -	6	7	2 Nullahs	fors.
Torroff - -	7	1	2 Nullahs	fors.
Putyajury -	6	6		
	285	0		

Names of Places.	diſtances in Miles and Furl.		Rivers and Nullahs to be croſſed.	ford or ferry.
(Bangah in Silhet, continued)	285	0		
Dinnarpour hills -	10	0		
Ulmulpour - -	6	6		
Monu River -	2	6	-	fer.
Rajahpour - -	13	2		
Dilleerbund -	9	3		
Juree River - -	14	0	-	ford
Latoo - -	16	0		
Bangah - - -	16	0	Cuſiara R.	ford
	373	1		
BANKIBAZAR. See Gowgatchy -	16	2		
BANSAH paſs				
Patcoom - - -	183	6		
Banſah paſs - -	10	2		
	194	0		
BAR. See Patna 1ſt road	362	5		
BARNAGORE -	4	7		
BAUGNAN. See Midnapour 2d road -	29	5		
BAULEAH. See Rungpour 1ſt road -	143	7		
BAUMEEN paſs. See Singboom 4th road	143	6		

Names of Places.	diſtances in Miles and Furl.		Rivers and Nullahs to be croſſed.	ford or ferry.
BEERCOOL. The particulars wanting				
BEJURA				
Hurringber, in Bangah road - - -	253	1		
Bejura - - -	5	0		
	258	1		
BELCUCHY. See Cauleah	202	0		
BENARES 1ſt road, by Patna and Buxar				
PATNA - -	400	2		
Dynapour - -	11	4		
Seerpour - -	4	0		
Moneab - - -	5	6		
Coilure Gaut -	8	0	Soane	ford
ARRAH - -	8	6		
Gudrajegunge -	9	0		
Billongtee - -	6	6		
Ranaſagur - -	4	6		
Nuaw - -	8	1		
Dumroy -	6	1		
Buxar - -	12	3		
The remainder of this road is not yet ſurveyed.				
BENARES 2d road, by Patna and Saſeram				
PATNA - - -	400	2		
Fulwary - - -	9	6		
Ruſtangunge -	6	2		
	416	2		

Names of Places.	distances in Miles	and Furl.	Rivers and Nullahs to be crossed.	ford or ferry.
(Benares 2d road, continued)	416	2		
Jugdispour - -	4	0		
Sadabad - - -	10	0		
Mawbellipour - -	8	0		
Arval - - -	7	0		
Ismaelpour - -	6	7		
Samsernagur - -	10	1		
Daoudnagur - -	5	1		
Harriergunge - -	4	5	Soane R.	ford
Durnyhaut - -	8	4		
Bawzer - -	7	3		
SASERAM -	6	6		
Saseagur - -	7	3		
Jehenabad - -	9	0		
Burrahuly - -	7	3		
Moneer - - -	6	2		
Sant - - -	6	6	Durgooty R.	ford
Nobutpour - -	8	3	Caramnassa R.	ford
Sadraza - - -	5	6		
Jagdeese - -	7	3		
Mogulserai - -	4	1		
BENARES - -	8	6	Ganges R.	fer.
	565	6		
BENARES 3d road by Gayah. Burdhoo or Bertha in Patna 3d road	271	3		
Siatgong - -	6	3		
Penuree - -	4	3	Nullah	ford
Merjapour - -	11	3	Ditto	ford
Nallabiga -	10	1		
Gayah - - -	10	7	Fulgo	ford
Kesaw - -	6	2		
Pachainpour -	4	6		
Tickarry - -	4	2		
Couch - -	4	6		
	334	4		

Names of Places.	diſtances in Miles and Furl.		Rivers and Nullahs to be croſſed.	ford or ferry.
(Benares 3d road, continued)	334	4		
Gow - - -	9	0		
Pattypour - -	10	6		
Daoudnagur - -	7	6		
BENARES, as before	98	3		
	460	3		
BERNAGUR. See Sooty 2d road - -	126	5		
BETTYAH 1ſt road by Patna				
PATNA - - -	400	2		
HAJYPOUR - -	4	6	Ganges R.	fer.
Singhyah - -	12	6		
Doudnagur - -	8	3		
Buſſunt - - -	7	0		
Golka - - -	8	1		
Sarungpour - -	6	4		
Karnoul - -	6	5		
Kiſſerya - - -	6	0	Byar N.	ford
Jeſſola - - -	7	4		
Ouluah - - -	6	0		
Lowyah - -	5	2		
Muckenya - -	8	6		
Beattee - -	10	5		
BETTYAH - -	1	6		
	500	2		
BETTYAH 2d road				
MONGHIR, in Patna 1ſt road - - -	300	6		
Bellya - -	9	6	Ganges R.	fer.
Low Cooty - -	11	0	Bogmutty R.	fer.
Monjowl - -	5	6		
Sacrowly - -	6	4		
Barriapour - -	6	1		
	339	7		

Names of Places.	distances in Miles and Furl.		Rivers and Nullahs to be crossed.	ford or ferry.
(Bettyah 2d road continued)	339	7		
Rampour - - -	8	0	Bogmutty R.	fer.
Nagorbussy - - -	13	0	Little Gunduck R	ford
Pusa - - -	12	2		
Sarubdypour - -	14	6		
Rowee - -	7	4	ditto	ford
Majufferpour -	3	3		
Mustasaggee - -	10	0	Little Gunduck	ford
Turki - -	5	6		
Mudwa - - -	8	6		
Maissey - -	6	0	ditto	ford
Naranpukry - -	9	0		
Chittamonpour -	5	4		
Gareea - - -	6	3		
Lowyah - -	7	5		
BETTYAH, as before	21	1		
	478	7		
BEYHAR, or Coos Beyhar. See Bugaduar	312	2		
BIRBOOM. See Nagore	131	0		
BIRKOOTY. See Patchwarry - - . -	149	3		
BISNEE				
Dumdum - -	6	0		
Baraset - -	7	4		
Amedunga - -	7	2	Nullah	ford
Jagoleah - -	9	1		
Hell, or Burrye -	4	4	Jubuna N.	ford
	34	3		

Names of Places.	distances in Miles and Furl.		Rivers and Nullahs to be crossed.	ford or ferry.
(Bishee continued)	34	3		
Chandpour - -	7	5	Nullah	ford
Runnagaut - -	5	4	Chournee R.	fer.
Barrasat - -	7	3	Nullah	ford
Taxal Ferry - -	3	1	Nullah	fer.
KISHENAGUR -	8	6		
Mohatpour - -	6	0		
Andulya - - -	9	4		
Putimahry - -	3	7	} Nullahs	fors.
Bettay - -	11	6	}	
Solamary - -	4	6		
Obipour - - -	8	0	Nullah	ford
Moshidunga - -	3	0	Boirub	ford
Jellinghee - -	10	2	Jellinghee R.	ford
Dyrampour - -	3	6	Nullah	ford
Surda - -	9	4	Ganges R.	fer.
Pootya - -	9	3	Barreyl & Narrud	fors.
NATTORE -	10	1		
Peeparool Gaut -	5	2	Barruly R.	fer.
Bangajungle - -	6	1	Goor R.	fer.
Pudser - - -	5	0		
Champapour -	8	3		
Ghiabunder - -	8	4	Nagore N.	ford
Punderaticky -	11	4		
Seebgunge - -	4	2	ditto	ford
Gobingunge - -	11	0	Currattya R.	fer.
Motra - -	4	3	Nullua N.	ford
Noongola -	9	4	Goggot R.	fer.
Barabuldya - -	8	4	Coolny R.	fer.
Pansgutchy -	8	0	Monaash R. twice	fors.
Olyapour - -	11	0	Teesta R.	fer.
Duregapour - -	5	4	Bamany N.	ford
Curygong - -	8	2		
Deenhotta -	7	6	Durla R.	fer.
Poonkur - -	10	5	Sunecoss R.	fer.
Harribanga - -	8	6	Nullah	ford
Dubarye -	3	2		
Mettabaug -	7	2	Gaddada R.	fer.
	309	3		

Names of Places.	distances in Miles	and Furl.	Rivers and Nullahs to be crossed.	ford or ferry.
(Bisnee continued)	309	3		
RANGAMATTY -	6	0	Nullah	ford
Farlee - - -	10	0	Sunecoss R.	fer.
Botagong - -	12	3	Gouroung R.	ford
Choutaaky - -	13	0		
Dangtola - -	9	0	Champomatty R.	fer.
Maashgong -	13	4		
Kanchdaw -	8	1	Barally R.	fer.
Bisnee - - -	6	0		
	387	3		
BISSUNPOUR. See Koondah - - -	86	4		
BOGARIAH. See Monghir 2d road -	247	6		
BOGLIPOUR				
1st road, by Terriagully. See Patna 1st road	263	0		
2d road, by Burdwan				
Chilkore, in Monghir 2d road - -	235	6		
Ruttungunge -	8	2		
BOGLIPOUR -	11	4		
	255	4		
BOGWANGOLA				
MOORSHEDABAD, in Patna 1st road -	118	5		
Cuttora - - -	2	0		
	120	5		

Names of Places.	distances in Miles and Furl.		Rivers and Nullahs to be crossed.	ford or ferry.
(Bogwangola continued)	120	5		
Palasbary -	5	1		
Baderpour -	4	3		
Bogwangola - -	5	0		
	135	1		
BONGONG. See Dacca	47	6		
BOOSNAH. See Jaffiergunge -	118	6		
BOWANIGUNGE. See Rungpour -	167	4		
BUDDAUL. See Rungpour	207	1		
BUDGEBUDGE. See Midnapour 2d road	13	4		
BUGGURA (Cutcherry of Shiberis)				
Champapour, in Bisnee road	181	3		
Tattah - -	5	6	Nagore N.	ford
Daguntah -	5	0		
Buggura - - -	8	0		
	200	1		
BULRAMPOUR				
Pertapour, in Singboom 1st road - - -	102	2		
Bulrampour -	8	4		
	110	6		

Names of Places.	distances in Miles and Furl.		Rivers and Nullahs to be croffed.	ford or ferry.
BURDWAN				
1ft road by Deneacally. See Patna 1ft road.	61	4		
2d road by Banfberrya				
Banfberrya, in Patna 1ft road	28	7	Nullah	fer.
Purrua - - -	10	2	Nullah	fer.
Boenchee - -	5	1		
Chatkundy - -	5	7		
Burfool - -	12	4		
BURDWAN -	7	6		
	70	3		
BURGANCOOTY				
Gobingunge, in Bifnee road	216	5		
Burgancooty -	2	0		
	218	5		
BURHAMPOUR Cantonments				
Daudpour, in Patna 1ft road	99	0		
Burrua - - -	3	7		
Moncara - -	7	2		
Burhampour -	4	0		
	114	1		
BURRABOOM				
Muccroo, in Patcoom road	146	7		
Burraboom - -	3	6		
	150	5		
BURRONHUTTY				
Dumdum - -	6	0		
Bolgatta - -	11	6		
Malletpour -	13	3		
Burronhutty - -	13	4		
	44	5		

Names of Places.	distances in Miles	and Furl.	Rivers and Nullahs to be croſſed.	ford or ferry.
BURWAH				
Petrabad, in Koonda road	200	7		
Sooteree - - -	6	6		
Sone - - - - -	6	5	Bera R.	ford
Coolee - - -	6	5		
Punchaw - - -	7	7		
Miſraw - - -	8	4		
Tilburrea - - -	5	2		
Ogidoo - - -	10	4		
Coolybunra - -	9	0		
* *DOSAH*, or *CHUTAH NAGPOUR* - -	24	0		
Moorguh - -	10	0		
Nowady - -	10	0	Coyle R.	ford
Kohtaum - -	8	0		
* Jaragi Paſs - -	9	0		
* Solamee - -	5	4		
* *BURWAH* -	7	4		
	336	0		
BUXADUAR Paſs, in Bootan				
RUNGPOUR - -	260	5		
Doomhaut - -	7	0	Monaaſh N.	ford
Saftybary - -	6	7	2 Nullahs	fors.
Mongulhaut - -	9	4		
Solmary - -	6	3	Durla R.	ford
Dinnahatta - -	3	5		
Belladinga - -	3	7		
Toreſha River -	5	3	- -	fer.
Mawamary - -	2	1		
COOS-BETHAR -	6	7		
Petajar Wood - -	5	4		
Bowanigunge - -	9	0	Surradinga R.	fer.
Chichacotta - -	4	0		
Randee Chowar -	6	4		
Santerabary - -	8	3		
* *Buxaduar* - -	10	0		
	355	5		

Names of Places.	diſtances in Miles and Furl.		Rivers and Nullahs to be croſſed.	ford or ferry.
BUXAR. See Benares 1ſt road	485	3		
BUXIGUNGE. See Rungpour - - -	222	3		
BUXIPOUR, in Mahmudſhi. See Seerpour 2d road	108	6		
BYGONBARY. See Suſung	247	0		
BYKONTPOUR				
Saibgunge, or *Raymgunge*, in Dellamcotta road	283	6		
Baccallyhaut - -	12	5	Goggot	ford
Baſſaſubahaut -	9	6		
Gopalgunge - -	5	6	Nulla	ford
Bykontpour - -	8	0	Teeſta R.	fer.
	319	7		
CANTALBARRY. See Luckiduar -	314	7		
CARAGOLA. See Purneah	238	0		
CAUGMAHRY. See Nulſhi Imaumpour	189	0		
CAULEAH				
Altyah, in Suſung road	183	4		

Names of Places.	distances in Miles and Furl.		Rivers and Nullahs to be crossed.	ford or ferry.
(Culeah continued)	183	4		
Suntosh - -	4	2	Lojung R.	fer.
Gundruckpour -	4	7	Joobnee R.	fer.
Belkuchy - -	9	3	Coni	fer.
Canleah - - -	8	4		
	210	4		
CHACKI, or Fort Hastings 1st road. See Patna 2d road -	215	1		
2d road				
Surya, in Patna 2d road	182	7		
Roonay - -	12	1		
Poonassy -	8	0		
Chacki - - -	9	2		
	212	2		
CHANDERCONA				
Ompta, in Midnapore 1st road - -	23	1	[Roopnaran	
Rajegur - -	13	4	Dummooda and	fers.
Gottaul - -	6	3	Selai R.	fer.
Radnagur - -	7	6		
Keerpoy - -	2	0		
Chandercona -	6	5	ditto	ford
	59	3		
CHANDERNAGORE. See Patna 1st road -	21	2		
CHANDPOUR. See Islamabad 1st road	191	5		
CHARCOLLY. See Baminy - -	149	7		

Names of Places.	distances in Miles and Furl.		Rivers and Nullahs to be crossed.	ford or ferry.
CHATMOL. See Seerpour 2d road -	158	0		
CHATNA. See Koonda	116	2		
CHICHACOTTA. See Buxaduar -	334	6		
CHILCORE. See Monghir 2d road - -	235	6		
CHILMARY				
Noongola, in Bisnee road	230	4	Goggot R.	fer.
Boggurya - -	7	0	Coolney R.	fer.
Nallagunge -	8	0	Serri R.	fer.
Chilmary - -	7	1	Teesta N.	ford
	252	5		
CHINSURA. See Patna 1st road				
Chandernagore -	21	2		
Chinsura - -	2	6		
	24	0		
CHITTAGONG. The same as Islamabad -	316	7		
CHOGDAH				
Hell, or Burrye, in Bisnee road - -	34	3		
Chogdah - -	7	0		
	41	3		

Names of Places.	distances in Miles	and Furl.	Rivers and Nullahs to be crossed.	ford or ferry.
CHOGONG. See Dewangunge 2d road -	175	0		
CHOWSAR				
Buxar, in Benares 1st road	485	3		
Chowsar - - -	6	6		
	492	1		
CHUNARGUR				
Mogulserai, in Benares 2d road - -	556	0		
Chunargur - -	18	0		
	574	0		
CHUPRAH. See Sewaan	436	1		
COLGONG, See Patna 1st road - -	243	4		
COLINDA. See Islamabad 1st road - -	249	3		
COMERCOLLY				
Aulumpour, in Seerpour 2d road - -	118	0		
Comercolly - -	10	6		
	128	6		
COMILLA. See Kundal	227	4		

Names of Places.	distances in Miles and Furl.		Rivers and Nullahs to be crossed.	ford or ferry.
CONCHON. See Nohutta, in Rungpour 1st road	151	4		
Dorole - - -	4	5		
Gosah - - -	5	2		
Doolabarry - -	9	6		
Limbobarya - -	8	0		
Maddapour - -	7	4	Attri R.	fer.
Conchon - - -	8	0		
	194	5		
CONSUMAGUNGE. See Dellamcotta - -	255	5		
COORSAH				
Saftybary, in Buxaduar road - - -	274	4		
Quoilagaut - -	6	3	Durla R.	fer.
Coorsah - - -	6	6	Neelcomer R.	fer.
	287	5		
COOSERAH. See Bahar 3d road - -	354	5		
COPPRAGUDDY Pass, See Singboom 1st road	176	5		
COSSIMBUZAR. See Patna 1st road -	116	2		
COTUMBAH. See Rotas Gur - - -	377	2		

Names of Places.	distances in Miles and Furl.		Rivers and Nullahs to be crossed.	ford or ferry.
CULNA (in Burdwan). See Patna 1st road -	51	6		
CULNA (in Jessore). See Backergunge 1st road	100	6		
CULPEE				
Balliah - - -	6	5		
Oderampour - -	7	7		
Atimnagur - -	3	6		
Monian - -	7	4		
Anorpour - -	7	0	Nullah	fer.
Culpee - - -	3	5		
	36	3		
CURRUCKDEA. See Patna 3d road - -	215	7		
CURRUCKPOUR 1st road. See Monghir 2d road - -	264	6		
2d road by Terriagully				
Pialapour, in Patna 1st road	232	0		
Buddlegunge - -	3	4		
Sowlee - - -	6	0		
Budeeah - - -	12	0		
Tirtcha - - -	4	6		
Ruttungunge - -	11	0	Chundun N.	ford
Sojowle - - -	2	5		
Gospour - - -	6	0		
Tarrapour - - -	8	6	Bunwa N.	ford.
CURRUCKPOUR -	7	4		
	294	1		

Names of Places.	distances in Miles	and Furl.	Rivers and Nullahs to be crossed.	ford or ferry.
CURRYBARRY Purgunnah It lies on the East-side of the Burrumpooter River, opposite Chilmary				
CURYGONG. See Bisnoe	271	6		
CUSTEE. See Seerpour 2d road - - -	127	6		
CUTTACK. See Ganjam	247	4		
CUTWA. See Patchwarry - - -	85	5		
DACCA 1st road				
Dumdum - -	6	0		
Baraset - - -	7	4		
Dottapugry - -	5	6		
Jawberrya - -	7	5		
Janapole - - -	3	7		
Mullickpour - - -	4	3	Jubuna N.	ford
Chanpara - -	6	5		
Bungong - - -	6	0	Issamot R.	fer.
Porabary - - -	5	6	2 Nullahs	fers.
Jaddopour - -	5	6	Nullah	fer.
Jingergutcha - -	7	0	Cobaduck R.	fer.
MOORLEY, or *JESSORE*	7	7	Nullah	ford
Neelgunge - - -	2	0	Boirub R.	fer.
Rajapour - - -	5	4		
	81	5		

Names of Places.	distances in Miles and Furl.		Rivers and Nullahs to be crossed.	ford or ferry.
(Dacca 1st road continued)	81	5		
Docallee - -	4	2	Sittareea R.	fer.
Gunagotta - -	8	6	Ditto	fer.
Nobatta - - -	7	6	Nowgonga R.	fer.
MAHMUDPOUR -	7	4		
Jaynagur - - -	7	3	Burrashee R.	fer.
Gopalpour - -	7	0	Comer R.	fer.
Furridpour - - -	8	6		
Hajygunge - - -	6	2		
Nurilapour - -	7	0	Ganges R.	fer.
Mynehaut - -	3	0		
Nabobgunge - -	7	2	Issamutty R.	fer.
Churan - - -	6	0		
Pattergotta - -	11	0	3 Nullahs	fers.
DACCA - - -	6	0	Dolaserry & Boorygonga Rs.	fers.
	179	4		
DACCA 2d road, direct from Hajygunge				
Hajygunge, as before -	139	2		
Mynehaut - -	10	0	Ganges R. & Hajygunge C.	fers.
Nabobgunge - -	7	2	Issamutty R.	fer.
Churan - - -	6	0	Nullah	fer.
Tagourpour - -	9	0	Issamutty & Dollaserry.	fers.
DACCA - - -	5	4	Boorygonga R.	fer.
	177	0		
DAOUDNAGUR				
1st road. See Patna 1st road - - -	467	3		
2d road. See Benares 3d road - -	362	0		

Names of Places.	distances in Miles	and Furl.	Rivers and Nullahs to be crossed.	ford or ferry.
DARRA, in Jungleterry, 1st road by Mobog Gaut				
NAGORE, in Patna 2d road - - -	131	0		
Lettabunny Gaut -	5	2		
Baharow - -	3	4	More R.	ford
Mobog Gaut - -	5	4		
Futtapour - -	4	0	Nullah	ford
Doomka - -	9	0		
Lagwoon - -	7	0		
Amerpour - -	6	0		
Noony - - -	5	4		
Kindooah - -	6	6		
Dunwa - - -	4	0		
Darra - - -	11	2		
	198	6		
DARRA 2d road, by Sarhaut				
Sarhaut, in Patna 2d road	171	3		
Gundajury - -	4	0		
Gurgurree - -	6	2		
Kyrabond - -	8	0		
Burgoo - - -	1	6		
Kindooah - -	8	4		
Dunwa - - -	4	0		
Darra - - -	11	2		
	215	1		
DARRA 3d road, by Deogur				
Cudhar, in Monghir 3d road - - -	209	2		
Luchmipour - -	3	4		
Durrampour - -	6	2		
Darra - - -	7	6		
	226	6		

Names of Places.	distances in Miles	and Furl.	Rivers and Nullahs to be crossed.	ford or ferry.
DELLAMCOTTA Fort, in Bootan				
MOORSHEDABAD, in Patna 1st road - -	118	5		
Bomineab - -	8	3		
Banniagong - -	4	3		
Sankral - - -	3	4	Nullah	ford
Meenkoot - -	4	4		
Godagary - -	3	0	Ganges R.	fer.
Nabobgunge - -	8	5		
Chappigunge - -	5	4		
Kesbah - - -	7	4		
Okilpour - -	7	0		
Daudpour - -	8	0		
Titalya - - -	4	6		
Nisbanpour - - -	8	4		
Dourgunge - - - -	7	3		
Nysinta - - -	10	2	Nullah	ford
Pransagur - -	10	2		
Ramsagur - -	7	2		
DINAGEPOUR, or *RAJE-GUNGE* - -	5	6	Nullah	ford
Cantoonagur - -	11	4	Nullah	ford
Consumahgunge - -	11	0	Teesta R.	fer.
Bowanygunge - -	5	0		
Dewangunge - -	11	3		
Mirzagunge - -	2	4		
Saibgunge, or *Raymgunge*	9	2	Goggot R.	ford
Beekrohaut - -	7	4	A Jeel	ford
Boutehaut - -	5	4		
Durega, or Doongahaut	7	4		
Bottabarry - -	4	3		
Fooljerra - -	9	0	Durla R.	ford
Kyranty - -	6	7		
Entrance of the Hills -	7	4	Ditto	ford
* Dellamcotta - -	15	0		
	344	4		

Names of Places.	distances in Miles and Furl.		Rivers and Nullahs to be crossed.	ford or ferry.
DENEACOLLY. See Patna 2d road - -	34	1		
DEOGUR. See Patna 2d road - - -	194	7		
DEOPOUR (near Serampour)				
Ayturah, in Patna 3d road	139	5		
Koolburryah - -	12	0		
Foolejury - -	10	6		
Koortah - -	8	1		
Deopour - -	13	0		
	183	4		
DEWANGUNGE, in Rungpour. See Dellamcotta - -	272	0		
DEWANGUNGE (in Patladaw) 1st road				
Seebgunge, in Bisnee road	205	5		
Curryabadder - -	13	0	Nullah C.	ford
Burradcally - -	9	0	Goggot R.	fer.
Dewangunge - -	12	0	2 Nullahs	fers.
	239	[illegible]		
DEWANGUNGE 2d road				
NATTORE, in Bisnee road - - -	156	5		
Gobinpour - -	5	0	Attri R.	fer.
Cullum - - -	6	5	Goor R. & a Nullah	fers.
	168	2		

Names of Places.	distances in Miles and Furl.		Rivers and Nullahs to be crossed.	ford or ferry.
(Dewangunge 2d road continued) - -	168	2		
Chogong - -	6	6		
Sukos - - -	7	2		
Pingher - - -	5	2		
Seerpour . - -	6	0	Curallya R.	ford
Caddi - - -	8	6	Issamutty N.	ford
Rogadow Gaut -	7	4	Monaash R.	fer.
Nokeela - - -	5	4		
Golabarry - - -	7	4		
Duremote - -	13	2	Nullah	ford
Dewangunge - -	10	1	3 Nullahs	fors.
	246	1		
DIGNAGUR. See Patna 2d road - -	81	4		
DINAGEPORE. See Dellamcotta - -	233	1		
DOARSINNY Pass. See Singboom 3d road - -	209	7		
DOBAGAUT, or Muncalgar Pass, in Birboom				
NAGORE - -	131	0		
Baharow - -	8	6		
Dobagaut - -	5	2		
	145	0		
DUGALHATTY				
Nogong, in Rungpour road	185	5		
Dugalhatty - -	3	0		
	188	5		
DUMROY Aurung				
Hajygunge, in Dacca road	139	2		

Names of Places.	distances in Miles and Furl.		Rivers and Nullahs to be crossed.	ford or ferry.
(Dumroy continued) -	139	2		
Burruacally - -	10	0	Ganges R. & a Nullah	fers.
Saapour - -	9	2	Issamutty R.	fer.
Bowanygunge - -	4	4		
Dumroy - -	8	0	Dollaserry R.	fer.
	171	0		
DURBUNGAH. See Seedley	376	1		
DUTTYAH JANGIERPOUR				
Tarwas, in Seerpour 2d road - - -	177	1		
Bobanganty Cutchery -	10	4		
	187	5		
DYNAPOUR Cantonments. See Benares 1st road	411	6		
ENGLISH BAZAR. See Purneah 2d road -	185	3		
FRINGYBAZAR. See Narrangunge - -	178	5		
FUTTAPOUR, in Darra road - - -	149	2		
GANJAM				
Surman's Bridge - -	2	7		
Budgebudge - -	10	5	2 Nullahs	
Seedsburrya - -	4	6	Hoogly R.	fer.
Pollerah - -	6	6		
	25	0		

Names of Places.	distances in Miles	and Furl.	Rivers and Nullahs to be crossed.	ford or ferry.
(Ganjam continued) -	25	0		
Baugnan - -	4	5	Dummoodah R.	fer.
Mauncore - -	5	0	2 Nullahs	fers.
Poobmanca - -	3	5	Roopnarrain R.	fer.
Conneadee - -	4	3		
Purtabpour, or *Cassai-jurab*	7	4		
Dogutchyab - -	8	0	Cossar or Catan N.	fer.
Kedaar - - -	6	4		
Bansychuck - -	5	0		
Badercally - -	5	0		
Narangur - -	5	3		
Cautnagur - -	5	6		
Dantoun - -	8	0		
Jellasore - -	12	7		
Raujegaut - -	3	6	Subanreeka R.	ford
Multanny - -	5	0		
Bustar - - -	6	4	Jumrai R.	
Gurpudda - -	3	0		
Ramchundrapour -	6	2		
Foolarra Gaut - -	5	5	Soane R.	fer.
Balasore - -	4	2		
Upurga Chokey -	8	2	Nullah	
Surow - - -	14	2	2 ditto	
Cansbaria Bridge -	4	5		
Rhanee's Tank -	9	5		
Budderuck - -	6	7	Sollundry R.	fer.
Daumnagur - -	11	0		
Jargepour - -	8	6	Gauitry R. 2 branches	
Burwa - - -	5	1	Nullah	
Cumery - -	4	7	Cumery R. 2 branches	
Harcapour - -	8	3	Jingotty R.	
Rachapour - - -	6	2		
Pudampour - -	11	0	Gobreah R.	
CUTTACK - -	7	4	Mahanudi	
	247	4		

Names of Places.	distances in Miles and Furl.		Rivers and Nullahs to be crossed.	ford or ferry.
(Ganjam continued) -	247	4		
Choaky - -	9	0		
Ballintash - -	4	4	Nullah	
Gopinatpour - -	9	6	Cudgery R.	fer.
Pieply - - -	4	1		
Amatpour - -	11	7		
Junicadpour - -	4	7	ditto	
Jagarnaut - -	7	0	ditto	
Narsingapatam - -	9	0	ditto	
Manickpatam - -	11	6	Chilka Lake	fer.
Muttacoona Choky -	8	4		
Maloud Choky -	12	0		
Poyah - - -	8	0		
Ganjam - - -	9	6		
	357	5		
GAREEAH Field. See Sooty 2d road - -	151	1		
GAYAH. See Benares 3d road - - -	314	4		
GENTIAH				
SILHET - -	325	3		
Chicknacole Hills - -	9	6		
Rannee ca Tallaw -	7	6		
GENTIAH - -	7	0	Nullah	ford
	349	7		
GHYRETTY. See Patna 1st road - -	16	7		

Names of Places.	distances in Miles and Furl.		Rivers and Nullahs to be crossed.	ford or ferry.
GOALPARA				
RANGAMATTY - -	315	3		
Dudekoar - -	17	0	Sunecoss R. Gourong	fer. ford
Jugbigopa - -	21	0	Champomatty R.	fer.
Goalpara - -	5	2	Burrampooter R.	fer.
	358	5		
GOBINGUNGE. See Bisnee - - -	216	5		
GODAGARY. See Dellamcotta - - -	142	3		
GONGACALLY				
Baugnan, in Midnapour 2d road - -	29	5		
Gongacally - -	13	4	Roopnaran R.	fer.
	43	1		
GOPAULGUNGE				
Kolna, in Backergunge 2d road - - - - - -	105	5	Nowgonga R.	fer.
Cajol - - -	9	6		2 fer.
Dungree - -	3	0		fer.
Gopaulgunge - -	4	6		2 fer.
	123	1		
GORAGOT. See Rungpour 2d road - -	232	3		
GOTTAUL. See Chanderconna - - -	43	0		

Names of Places.	distances in Miles and Furl.		Rivers and Nullahs to be croffed.	ford or ferry.
GOUR Ruins				
Nabobgunge, in Dellamcotta road - -	151	0		
Seebgunge - -	11	0	Mahanada R.	fer.
Pookarya - -	4	6		
Habafconna Gaut, in *Gour*	11	2		
	178	0		
GOWGATCHY				
Barnagur - -	4	7		
Sookfor - - -	4	7		
Bankibazar - -	6	4		
Gowgatchy - -	3	2		
	19	4		
GUBINAGUR. See Sanafhygotta - -	266	6		
GUIDORE. See Patna 2d road - - -	243	3		
GURNADY. See Backergunge 2d road -	165	3		
GUZGOTTA				
RUNGPOUR - -	260	5		
Guzgotta - -	7	4		
	268	1		
GWAREE. See Moorfhedabad 2d road -	68	6		

Names of Places.	Distances in Miles and Furl.		Rivers and Nullahs to be crossed.	ford or ferry.
HAJYGUNGE. See Dacca	139	2		
HAJYPOUR. See Bettyah 1st road - - -	405	0		
HARRIERPOUR. See Soojanhy Pass - -	141	1		
HENDOOAH, or Herboe. See Noony - -	175	6		
HOBIBGUNGE. See Backergunge 2d road -	143	5		
HOBITNAGUR				
Sagordy, in Laour road	227	7		
Agarasondu - -	3	0	Burrampooter R.	fer.
Hobitnagur - -	14	2		
	245	1		
HOOGLY. See Patna 1st road - - -	25	5		
HULDIPOOKRE. See Singboom - -	178	0		
HURRYAL. See Seerpour 2d road - -	168	0		

Names of Places.	distances in Miles and Furl.		Rivers and Nullahs to be crossed.	ford or ferry.
HYDERABAD. The same as Soory - -	115	3		
JAFFIERGUNGE				
MAHMUDPOUR, in Dacca road - -	110	0		
Boosnah - -	8	6	Burrashee R.	fer.
Nulluah - -	6	4	Comer N.	ford
Cameldiggy - -	10	2	Harrigonga N.	ford
Patral - - -	9	1		
Jaffiergunge - -	5	6	Ganges R.	fer.
	150	3		
JAGRENAUT. See Ganjam - - -	298	5		
JALALGUNGE				
Burradirga, in Rungpour 2d road - -	253	3		
Jalalgunge - -	8	0		
	261	3		
JANGUIRA. See Patna 1st road - - -	279	7		
JANPOUR. See Soojanhy Pass - - -	103	7		
JARBARRY				
Cantoonagur, in Dellamcotta road - -	244	5		
Gurnabary - - -	11	4	Teesta R.	fer.
Jarbarry - - - -	5	5		
	261	6		

Names of Places.	diſtances in Miles and Furl.		Rivers and Nullahs to be croſſed.	ford or ferry.
JAULDOE. See Junoh Paſs	192	3		
JAYNAGUR. See Dacca	117	3		
JELLASORE. See Ganjam	106	5		
JELLINGHY. See Biſnee	123	7		
JELPIGORY				
Baccally haut, in Bykontpour road - -	296	3		
Jelpigory - -	6	7		
	303	2		
JENNIDAH				
Jingergutcha, in Dacca road	66	2		
Solahaut - -	9	0		
Candy - - -	4	2	Boirub R.	ford
NULDINGAH - -	10	4	Sittarya R.	ford
Jennidah - -	8	2	Nowgonga R.	ford
	98	2		
JESSORE. See Dacca	74	1		
JOYPOUR. See Junoh Paſs	177	3		
INDOS				
Jahanabad, in Koondah road - - -	50	7		
Akeluckeer - -	8	0	Dalkiſor R.	ford
Indos - - -	12	3		
	71	2		

Names of Places.	distances in Miles	and Furl.	Rivers and Nullahs to be crossed.	ford or ferry.
INJELLY. Particulars wanted				
INCHACOLUS. See Punduah - - -	329	1		
JOOGDYAH				
Colinda, in Islamabad road	249	3		
Joogdyah - -	8	4		
	257	7		
ISLAMABAD, or Chittagong				
Jaynagur, on the Dacca road	117	3		
Gordee - - -	6	2		
Tollumah or Talmah -	7	4		
Rajapour - -	10	0	Harvilla R.	fer.
Pulyculla - -	8	0	Nullah	fer.
Noorpour - -	6	4	Ganges R. & a Nullah	fers.
Dunconya - -	12	0	Nullah	fer.
Rajabarry - -	12	0		
Chandpour, by water -	12	0	Megna R.	fer.
Chandrahaut - -	11	0		
Buxyhaut - -	10	0	Dackitya R.	fer.
Luckipour - -	7	0		
Bibby Bazar - -	4	0	Nullah	fer.
Hazerypara - -	8	2		
Chandergunge - -	2	5	Nullah	ford
Currimpour - -	7	2	Nullah	ford
Colinda - - -	7	5		
Cassidya - -	8	7	Little Fenny R.	fer.
Meerjapour - -	4	7		
Fenny River - -	3	0	- -	fer.
Jurilgunge - -	5	6		
Meercaserai - -	7	0		
	278	7		

Names of Places.	distances in Miles	and Furl.	Rivers and Nullahs to be crossed.	ford or ferry.
(Islamabad continued)	278	7		
Seetacoon - -	12	4		
Comareeah - -	8	4	Nullah	br.
Cuddumrusil - -	5	0		
Jaffierabad - -	5	0		
ISLAMABAD - -	7	0		
	316	7		
ISLAMABAD 2d road by Dacca				
DACCA - -	179	5		
Futtulah - -	6	5	2 Nullahs	fer.
Naraingunge - -	2	6		
Gudjaleah - -	7	2	3 ferries	fer.
Allynya - - -	9	0	2 Nullahs & Megna R.	fers.
Coweddy - -	9	0	Gomut R.	fer.
Charratbanga - -	5	1	Nullah	ford
Chandrahaut - -	2	6	2 Nullahs	fers.
Gunganagur - -	8	5		
Beigypour - -	5	6		
Monahargunge - -	6	4	Dackitya N°.	fer.
Addarah - -	6	2		
Delluah - -	6	3		
Mahmud Ally-haut -	10	2	Little Feny R.	fer.
Meerjapour - -	11	7		
Fenny R.	3	0	- -	fer.
ISLAMABAD, as before	50	6		
	331	4		
ISLAMABAD Purgannah				
Seebgunge, in Bisnee road	205	5		
Curryabadder - -	13	0	Nullah	ford
Tengua Cutchery -	8	0	Bangalla R.	fer.
	226	5		

Names of Places.	distances in Miles and Furl.		Rivers and Nullahs to be crossed.	ford or ferry.
JUMDAY. See Mongher 2d road - -	237	4		
JUGHIGOPA. See Goalpara - - -	353	3		
JUMMU-CANDY				
Cutwa, in Patchwarra road	85	5		
Dautbuditya - -	8	5		
Talgong - - -	7	5	Queyah R.	fer.
Jummu-Candy - -	6	6		
	108	5		
JUNGLEBARRY. See Laour - - -	249	5		
JUNOH Pass, in Chuta Nagpour				
Chunditulla - -	12	0	Hoogly R. & 2 Nullahs	fers.
Adawmpour -	9	3		
Rajbulhaut -	9	0		
Chunderbaun -	7	4	Dummooda R.	ford
Dewangunge -	9	2	Dalkisor R.	ford
Ramjavenpour -	10	3		
Mongulputta - -	11	5	Selai R.	ford
Betah - - -	5	0		
Kistnagur - -	7	0	Ditto twice	fors
Parentool - -	10	5		
Taldingra - -	6	4		
Osburrea - -	13	6	Ditto	ford
Lolbazar - -	7	4		
Pyratelly - -	6	0		
Manboom - -	3	3	Cassai R.	ford
	128	7		

Names of Places.	distances in Miles	and Furl.	Rivers and Nullahs to be crossed.	ford or ferry.
(Junboh Pass continued)	128	7		
Jettajoory - -	4	3		
Juggela - -	7	6		
Ningur - - -	4	0		
Chacultury - -	9	3		
Rogonatgunge -	12	0		
Joypour - -	11	0	Cassai R	ford
Jauldoe - -	15	0		
Sillee - - -	12	0		
Junboh Pass - -	14	0		
	218	7		
KARNOUL. See Bettyah 1st road - -	454	3		
KEERPOY. See Chander-conna - -	52	6		
KINDOOA. See Darra	183	4		
KISHENAGUR. See Bisnee	66	6		
KOONDAH				
Chunditulla - -	12	0	Hoogly R. & 2 Nullahs	fers.
Adaumpour - -	9	3		
Rajbulbaut - -	9	0		
Chunderbaun -	7	4	Dummuda R.	ford
Jahanabad - -	13	0	Dalkisor R.	ford
Cuttool - -	10	5		
Cuttoolpour - -	4	2		
	65	6		

Names of Places.	distances in Miles	and Furl.	Rivers and Nullahs to be crossed.	ford or ferry.
(Koondah continued)	65	6		
Badgehaut - -	10	6		
BISSUNPOUR -	10	0		
Oondah - -	8	0		
Raujehaut - -	8	4	Dalkisor R.	ford
Duidgong - -	9	2		
Chatna - - -	4	0		
Tilnar - - -	6	4		
Rampour - -	9	1		
ROGONATPOUR -	11	4		
Domercola - -	4	3		
* Purseah - -	9	5		
Byra - - -	4	7	Guy N.	ford
Jubbra - - -	9	0		
Naranpour - -	8	5		
Radnagur - -	5	2		
Cosmar - -	10	1		
Petrabad - -	5	5		
* *Goleeah*, or Golah - -	8	4		
* *RAMGUR* - -	12	0	Dummooda R.	
* Jewry Gaut - -	20	0		
* Bulliah - -	8	0		
* Puggar - - -	13	4		
* Pudumpour - -	10	0		
* Bugra - - -	9	2		
Sebrajepour - -	4	4		
Singpour - -	6	0		
Koondah - -	11	0		
	303	5		
KUNDAL				
Noorpour, in Islamabad road - - -	155	5		
Duckinchargong -	13	0		
Idrackpour - -	12	0		
Gudjalea - -	4	2	Issamutty R.	fer.
	184	7		

Names of Places.	distances in Miles	and Furl.	Rivers and Nullahs to be crossed.	ford or ferry.
(Kundal continued) -	184	7		
Daoudcandy - -	9	6	2 Nullahs & Megna R.	fers.
Gowrypour - -	5	2	Gomut R.	
Gopalpour, or Gopalnagur	6	2		
Burcumpta - -	10	0		
Awmtulla - -	7	1		
COMILLAH - -	4	2		
Boggasi - -	12	3		
Choudagong - -	6	2		
Kundal - - -	12	0		
	258	1		
KYRANTY. See Dellamcotta - - -	324	4		
LACARACOONDA				
Dubragepour, in Patna 2d road - - -	117	4		
Lacaracoonda - -	8	6		
	126	2		
LAOUR				
DACCA - -	179	5		
Molaparah - -	9	7	Balloo N. & Luckia R.	fers.
Ballyah - -	2	3		
Saatgong - -	6	6		
Panchdownah - -	3	2		
Perralya - -	6	0	Burrampooter N.	ford
Dulcheddy - -	10	4		
Sagordee - -	9	4	Burrampooter R.	fer.
Dooldya - -	13	0	Nullah	fer.
Junglebarry - -	8	6	Nursundy N.	ford
Bowalhaut - -	10	0	Ditto	ford
	259	5		

Names of Places.	distances in Miles and Furl.		Rivers and Nullahs to be crossed.	ford or ferry.
(Laour continued) -	259	5		
Cundyeura - -	7	3	Nullah	ford
Soonajura - -	9	3	Moggura R.	fer.
Dowtan - - -	9	1	Cungas R.	fer.
Aatcapara - -	4	5	Nullah	fer.
Sookar - - -	7	7	Coyra and Bolee Rs.	fers.
Jamalgur - -	9	5	2 Nullahs	fers.
Laour - - -	5	0		
	312	5		
LUCKIDUAR				
Dewangunge, in Dellamcotta road - -	272	0		
Saibgunge or *Raymgunge*	11	6	Goggot R.	ford
Chingrabanda -	9	6		
Bogarbarry haut -	8	3	Durla R.	ford
* *Cantelbarry* - -	13	0	Jerdecker & Manshi Rs.	fords
Guntong - -	10	4	Moojenny R.	ford
Jaygong - -	8	4		
Cuballapara - -	3	0		
Luckiduar - -	7	0		
	343	7		
LUCKIPOUR. See Islamabad - - -	219	5		
LUCKIPOUR, in Bootan				
Guntong, in Luckiduar road - - -	325	1		
Injerra - - -	14	0		
Luckipour - -	6	4		
	345	5		

Names of Places.	diſtances in Miles and Furl.		Rivers and Nullahs to be croſſed.	ford or ferry.
LUCHMIPOUR, in Jungle-terry. See Darra 3d road	212	6		
LUSKERPOUR. See Pootya, in Biſnee road	146	4		
MADDAPOUR (Cutchery of Janguirpour). See Conchon - -	186	5		
MAHMUDPOUR. See Dacca - -	110	0		
MAHRAJEGUNGE				
MAULDAH, in Purneah 2d road - - -	188	6		
Purruah - -	7	2		
Mynah - - -	12	6		
Bygongong - -	10	5		
Meerjaſerra - -	6	7		
Himtabads - -	11	3		
Bindole - -	8	0	Coolick N.	ford
Taujepore - -	8	3	Nagore R.	ford
Kimpour - -	8	3		
Ballygurra - -	7	0		
Cograh - - -	6	0		
Mahrajegunge -	2	4		
	277	7		
MAISSEY. See Bettyah 2d road - - -	429	2		
MANBOOM. See Junoh Paſs - - -	128	7		

Names of Places.	distances in Miles and Furl.		Rivers and Nullahs to be crossed.	ford or ferry.
MANGY. See Suagra	447	5		
MAULDAH. See Purneah 2d road - -	188	7		
MEENKOOT. See Dellamcotta - -	139	3		
MIDNAPOUR				
Jurah - - -	7	6	Hoogly R. & 1 Nullah	fers.
Peniara - -	5	1		
Manickpeer Dirga -	4	4		
Omptah - - -	5	6		
Maunkore - -	8	6	Dummoodah R.	fer.
Poobmanca - -	3	5	Roopnaran R.	fer.
Pansbariah - -	8	3		
Nabobgunge - -	4	4		
Cawastagry - -	9	3	Cassai R.	fer.
Dogatchy - -	8	4		
MIDNAPOUR -	8	2		
	74	4		
MIDNAPOUR 2d road, by Baugnan				
Surman's Bridge -	2	7		
Budgebudge - -	10	5	2 Nullahs	
Seedsbarya -	4	6	Hoogly R.	fer.
Pollerah - -	6	6		
Baugnan - -	4	5	Dummoodah R.	fer.
Mauncore - -	5	0	2 Nullahs	fers.
MIDNAPOUR, as before	42	5		
	77	2		

Names of Places.	diſtances in Miles	and Furl.	Rivers and Nullahs to be croſſed.	ford or ferry.
MIRJANAGORE. See Backergunge - -	63	5		
MIRZAGUNGE				
Sutalury - -	150	5		
* *Mirzagunge* - -	24	0		
	174	5		
MOBOG Gaut, or Paſs. See Darra 1ſt road -	145	2		
MOISHPOUR. See Patchwarry - -	154	3		
MONGHIR				
1ſt road. See Patna 1ſt road - -	300	6		
2d road, by Birboom [the beſt]				
Deogur, in Patna 2d road	194	7		
Chandun Nullah -	10	3	- -	ford
Cudhar - - -	4	0		
Jumday - - -	8	4		
Bogarya - -	10	2		
Chilkore - -	7	6		
Noorgunge - -	1	3		
Kinwar - -	5	0		
Belharee - -	6	4		
Tarrapour - -	6	5	Burwa N.	ford
CURRUCKPOUR	7	4		
Paharpour - -	9	4		
Rampour - -	7	0		
MONGHIR	6	0		
	285	2		

Names of Places.	distances in Miles and Furl.		Rivers and Nullahs to be crossed.	ford or ferry.
MONGHIR				
3d road, by Rota, or Ratta Pass				
Deogur, as before - -	194	7		
Chandun - -	9	3	Nullah	ford
Cutterya - -	10	0	ditto	ford
Cosmow - -	10	0		
Rota Pass - -	9	2		
Chajura - -	4	0		
Gulnee - -	4	0		
Tarrapour - -	3	6	Bunwa N.	ford
MONGHIR, as before	30	0		
	275	2		
MONGULKOTE				
BURDWAN - -	61	4		
Mussundy - -	8	0		
Saggrah - -	3	6	Curree N.	ford
Arrawah - -	4	1		
Mongulkote - -	4	6		
	82	1		
MOODUPOUR, in Pookareeah. See Susung	218	0		
MOORLEY, or Jessore. See Dacca - -	74	1		
MOORSHEDABAD, or Mootyjyl 1st road. See Patna	118	5		

Names of Places.	distances in Miles and Furl.		Rivers and Nullahs to be crossed.	ford or ferry.
MOORSHEDABAD 2d road, by Kishenagur				
KISHENAGUR, in Bisnee road - - - -	66	6		
Gwabree - -	2	0		
Niahaut - -	7	2	Jellinghy R.	ford
Jugdanpour - -	7	7		
Bickrampour - -	3	6		
Pangotta - -	7	0	Nullah	ford
Plassey - - -	5	6		
MOORSHEDABAD, as before - - -	26	1		
	126	4		
MULFUTGUNGE				
Noorpour, in Islamabad road - - -	155	5		
Nunkissergunge -	13	6	Nullah	ford
Mulfutgunge - -	8	2	Calligonga R.	fer.
	177	5		
MUSTAN Gur				
Ghiabundar, in Bisnee road	189	7		
Mustan Gur - -	12	7		
	202	6		
NABOBGUNGE. See Dellamcotta - -	151	0		
NAGORBUSSY. See Bettyah 2d road - -	360	7		
NAGORE, or Birboom 1st road. See Patna 2d road - -	131	0		

Names of Places.	distances in Miles	and Furl.	Rivers and Nullahs to be crossed.	ford or ferry.
NAGORE				
2d road, by Soory				
Curnagore, as before	93	2		
Rupour - - -	6	5	Adji R.	ford
Coostigerya - -	8	3		
Comah - - -	5	4	Baccasore N.	ford
Soory, or *Hyderabad* -	4	7		
Dulebpour Gaut -	8	3		
NAGORE - -	7	5		
	134	5		
CHUTA-NAGPOUR, or *DOESAH*. See Burwa	286	0		
NARANGUNGE				
Duckinchargong, in Kundal road - -	168	5		
Fringybazar - -	10	0		
Narangunge - -	3	1	Issamutty R. & 1 Nullah	fers.
	181	6		
NARANGUR. See Ganjam - - -	80	0		
NARANPOUR Aurung				
Chandpour, in Islamabad road - - -	191	5		
Mutlupgunge -	10	4	2 Tide Creeks	
Naranpour - -	4	6		
	206	7		
NARSINGUR. See Singboom - -	143	0		

Names of Places.	distances in Miles	and Furl.	Rivers and Nullahs to be crossed.	ford or ferry.
NATTORE. See Bisnee	156	5		
NAUTPOUR. See Ammerpour - -	308	6		
NISHANPOUR. See Dellamcotta - -	192	2		
NOBUTPOUR. See Benares 2d road -	539	6		
NOGONG. See Rungpour 1st road - -	185	5		
NOONY, or Hendooah 1st road. See Darra 1st road - -	175	6		
2d road				
Burgoo, in Darra 2d road	191	3		
Noony - - -	7	5		
	199	0		
NOORNAGUR				
Gowrypour, in Kundal road - - -	199	7		
Saliacondy - -	6	0	Nullah	ford
Tulah - - -	9	4	Gomut R.	fer.
Mokimpour - -	7	0	Nullah	ford
Noornagur - -	9	0	Nullah	ford
	231	3		
NORUNGAH. See Rotas Gur - - -	363	3		

Names of Places.	distances in Miles and Furl.		Rivers and Nullahs to be crossed.	ford or ferry.
NOTAGUR Pass. See Singboom - -	148	4		
NOWADAH. See Patna 3d road - -	274	3		
NOWGONG. See Seerpour 2d road - -	171	0		
NUDDEAH				
Summutgur, in Patna road	59	7		
Nuddeah - -	5	4	Nullah	ford
	65	3		
NULDINGAH. See Jennidah - -	90	0		
NULLUAH				
Raspugly - -	6	4		
Damoitulla - -	6	0		
Barrypour - -	5	4		
Bennypour - -	7	1	3 Nullahs	fors
Bessinpour - -	7	2	1 ditto	ford
Nulluah - -	4	0	1 ditto	fer.
	36	3		
NULSHI Imaumpour				
Attyah, in Susung road	183	4		
Caugmahry - -	5	4	Lojung R.	fer.
Potul - - -	9	7	2 Nullahs	fors
Nulshi - - -	7	0	Joobnee R.	fer.
	205	7		

Names of Places.	distances in Miles and Furl.		Rivers and Nullahs to be croſſed.	ford or ferry.
NURILAPOUR, See Dacca	146	2		
OKERAH, or Seergur. See Patna 3d road -	116	5		
OLIAPOUR. See Biſnee	258	0		
OMPTAH. See Midnapour	23	1		
OUDANULLAH. See Patna	184	3		
PACHETE 1ſt road				
Tilnar, in Koonda road	122	6		
Panchmool - -	9	6		
Saterrah - -	3	4		
PACHETE - -	5	2		
-	141	2		
PACHETE 2d road				
BURDWAN - -	61	4		
Belkoſs - -	5	5		
Daudpour - -	6	2		
Gopaulpour - -	7	2		
Futtypour - -	8	0		
Selimpour - -	6	1		
Nuddeah - -	8	5		
Serampour - - -	11	2		
Mudjeah - -	6	1	Dummooda R.	ford
Hannuah - -	9	0		
Barratpour - -	7	1		
PACHETE - -	9	3		
	146	2		

Names of Places.	distance in Miles and Furl.		Rivers and Nullahs to be crossed.	ford or ferry.
PALAMOW				
RAMGUR, in Koonda road - - -	221	3		
* Chuttapaloo Pass -	12	0		
* Chuttyah - -	12	0		
* Omedundah - -	14	0		
* Churiah - -	17	0		
* *Tikoo* - - -	12	4		
Tissia Pass - -	12	0		
Kurrya - - -	6	4		
* Monkeary - -	13	0		
* Monka - - -	15	0		
* *PALAMOW* - -	10	0		
	345	3		
PALGUNGE				
Serampour, in Patna 3d road - - -	191	5		
Palgunge - -	8	0	Burracur R.	ford
	199	5		
PARADANGA				
Deenhotta, in Bisnee road	279	4		
Paradanga - -	4	6		
	284	2		
PATCHWARRY				
Summutgur, in Patna road	59	7		
Muxipoogry - -	11	0		
Boxah - -	5	2		
Cutwa - - -	9	4		
Kiowgong - -	8	0	Adji R.	ford
Tarrapour - -	11	6	Queyah R.	fer.
Moneegong - -	7	3	More R.	ford
Boudgong - - -	12	6		
Margong - -	5	2		
	130	6		

Names of Places.	diſtances in Miles and Furl.		Rivers and Nullahs to be croſſed.	ford or ferry.
(PATCHWARRY continued)	130	6		
Nulbatty - -	10	0	2 Nullahs	fors.
Birkooty - - - -	9	5		
Egwarbary - -	3	0		
Moiſhpour - -	1	0		
Utcherya - - -	5	0		
Patchwarry - -	13	2	Banſli R.	ford
	172	5		
PATCOOM				
Manboom, in Junoh road	128	7		
Mudjehara - -	10	0		
Muccroo - -	8	0		
Luckenpour - -	8	0		
Malkee - - -	9	0		
Muroo - -	8	1		
Muſſera - -	6	6	Subunreka R.	ford
Patcoom - -	5	0		
	183	6		
PATGONG				
Dewangunge, in Dellamcotta road - -	275	0		
Sibegunge - -	11	6		
Patgong - -	12	0		
	298	6		
PATNA 1ſt road, by Moorſhedabad - -				
Barnagur - -	4	7		
Sookſor - -	4	7		
Ghyretty cantonments	7	1	Hoogly R.	fer.
Chandernagore - -	4	3		
HOOGLY - -	4	3		
	25	5		

Names of Places.	distances in Miles and Furl.		Rivers and Nullahs to be croſſed.	ford or ferry.
(PATNA continued)	25	5		
Banſbaria - -	3	2		
Niaſerai - -	4	4	2 Nullahs	fers.
Inchura - -	8	7		
Ambooah - -	6	6		
Culna - - -	2	6		
Merzapour - -	4	0	Nullah	fer.
Summutgur - -	4	1		
Jahanagur - -	4	2		
Beltully - -	7	2		
Pattolee - -	3	7		
Augurdeep - -	3	0	Coſſimbuzar R.	ford
Plaſſey - -	14	2		
Daudpour - -	6	4		
Burrua - -	3	7		
Chunapour - -	10	4		
COSSIMBUZAR -	2	7		
Mootyjyl (MOORSHEDABAD) - -	2	3	Coſſimbazar R. twice	fers.
Bomineah - -	8	3		
Dewanſerai - -	8	0		
Comra - -	10	4	Nullah	ford
Sooty - - -	8	2	Coſſimbuzar R.	ford
Downapour - -	11	1	2 Nullahs	fors.
Furruckaband -	7	6	Nullah	ford
Oudanulla - -	11	6		
RAJEMAL - -	6	4		
Muſſaw - -	10	0		
Sicklygully - -	9	3		
Gongaperſad - -	8	2		
Terriagully - -	4	4		
Shawabad - -	3	0		
Pialapour - -	6	0		
Colgong - -	11	4	Nullah	ford
Teermahony Nullah -	3	2	- -	fer.
Goga Nullah -	5	2	- -	fer.
	252	0		

Names of Places.	distances in Miles	and Furl.	Rivers and Nullahs to be crossed.	ford or ferry.
(PATNA continned)	252	0		
BOGLIPOUR - -	11	0		
Champernagur - -	2	3		
Sultangunge -	12	1	Nullah	ford
Janguira - -	2	3		
Georgut Nullah -	4	1	- -	fer.
Seetacoon - -	11	6		
MONGHIR - -	5	0		
Singhyah Nullah -	7	0	- -	ford
Surajegurra - -	10	6		
Rampour - -	7	5		
Jaintpour - -	7	5	3 Nullahs	1 fer 2 for
Doomarra - -	4	0		
Derriapour - -	6	1		
Shunar - -	5	5		
Punerack - -	7	4		
Bar - -	5	5		
Semmya - -	9	4		
Mogulpurra - -	8	3		
Bykuntpour - -	6	3		
Futwa - -	4	5		
PATNA - -	8	6		
	400	2		

Names of Places.	distances in Miles	and Furl.	Rivers and Nullahs to be crossed.	ford or ferry.
PATNA 2d road, by Birboom, and the Chacki pass				
Chunditullah - -	12	0	Hoogly R. & a Nullah	fer.
Bundipour - -	12	1		
Deneacolly - -	10	0		
Selimabad - -	10	2	Nullah	ford
Purlah - -	7	7		
Pyowrah - -	5	6		
BURDWAN factory -	3	4		
Bunpass - -	12	6	Curree N.	ford
	74	2		

Names of Places.	distances in Miles and Furl.		Rivers and Nullahs to be crossed.	ford or ferry.
(PATNA continued) -	74	2		
Dignagur - -	7	2		
Ousgong - -	6	2		
Curnagore - -	5	4		
Illambazar - -	7	0	Adji R.	ford
Gowrah - - -	9	6		
Kistnagur - -	4	3	Cupi N.	ford
Dubragepour - -	3	1		
Niagaut - -	6	7		
NAGORE, or *BIRBOOM*	6	5		
Doodapauny - -	5	5		
Doley - - -	5	3		
Asnah - - -	11	3		
Operbanda - -	10	0		
Sarhaut - -	8	0		
Surya - - -	11	6		
Deogur, or Deugur -	11	6		
Sirsah - - -	4	2		
Silpherry - -	8	0		
Asnah - - -	4	4		
Chacki, or Fort Hastings	3	6		
Betteah Gaut - -	7	2		
Dumree - - -	6	2		
Sonah - - -	2	4		
Jundoo - - -	4	4		
Guidore - - -	7	4		
Letchwar - -	13	0		
Islamnagur - -	6	4		
Dummoul - -	5	6		
Chuckwa - -	12	2		
Cuttree - - -	3	2	Sacry N.	ford
BAHAR - -	12	6	Panchanny N.	ford
Suan - - -	10	4	Banoura N.	ford
Hilsah - - -	10	0	2 Nullahs	fors.
Futwa - - -	14	6	Mahany R.	ford
PATNA - -	8	6		
	340	7		

H

Names of Places.	Distances in Miles	and Furl.	Rivers and Nullahs to be crossed.	ford or ferry.
PATNA 3d road, by Curruckdeah				
Dignagur, as before	81	4		
Mauncore - -	7	3		
Cookſee - -	6	4		
Gopalpour - -	5	6		
Puralya - -	9	4		
Okerah, or *Seetgur* -	6	0		
Rajahpour - -	10	4		
Ayturah - -	12	4		
Burmoory - -	7	4	Burracur R.	ford
Paunraw - -	6	6		
Debbe Yanna - -	3	0		
Hurkuttah - -	9	5		
Gadee Toonry -	10	5		
Panreedy - -	3	6	Ditto	ford
Serampour - -	10	6		
Burau - - -	6	4		
Nowada - -	11	4		
Curruckdeah - -	6	2		
Kiſgoe - - -	10	3		
Soank - - -	8	6	Sacry N. thrice	fors.
Gomah - - -	4	6	Ditto twice	fors.
Seebpour - -	13	6	Ditto thrice	fors.
Govinpour - -	6	4		
Baggor, or Delour Gaut	4	4	Ditto twice	fors.
Burdhoo - -	6	7		
Nowadah - -	3	0	Coory N.	ford
Gereek - - -	10	5	Ditto	ford
BAHAR - - -	11	1		
PATNA, as before -	44	0		
	340	1		
PAUNRAW. See Patna 3d road - -	153	6		

Names of Places.	distances in Miles and Furl.		Rivers and Nullahs to be crossed.	ford or ferry.
PERSAH				
BETTYAH - -	500	2		
Muttcah - -	18	0		
Kourbogga - -	14	0		
Rampour - -	10	0		
Persah - - -	8	0		
	550	2		
PIPLEY				
Jellasore, in Ganjam road	106	5		
Burrapol - -	8	3		
Pipley - - -	4	5		
	119	5		
PLASSEY. See Patna 1st road - - -	92	5		
POINTY. See Purneah 1st road - - -	231	0		
POOTYAH, in Luskerpour. See Bisnee - -	146	4		
PUBNA-NAZIRPOUR. See Seerpour 2d road -	137	6		
PUCCULOE				
Gwalpara, in Susung road	163	4		
Latoora - - -	11	0	Conoi R.	ford
PUCCULOE - -	6	6		
	181	2		

Names of Places.	diſtances in Miles and Furl.		Rivers and Nullahs to be croſſed.	ford or ferry.
PUNDUAH				
Agna, in Silhet road -	295	1		
Nabobgunge - -	10	6	2 Nullahs	fors.
Ruſſlgunge - -	4	6	1 ditto	ford
Digley - - -	9	6	1 ditto	fer.
Inchacolus - -	8	6	2 ditto	fors.
* *Pundua* - -	8	0	Soorma R.	fer.
	337	1		
PURNEAH 1ſt road, by Terriagully				
Terriagully, in Patna 1ſt road - - -	223	0		
Pointee - - -	8	0		
Caragola - -	7	0	Ganges R.	fer.
Gondwarra - -	14	0		
Milkee - - -	11	2		
PURNEAH - -	7	3		
	270	5		
PURNEAH 2d road, by Mauldah				
Chappigunge, in Dellamcotta road - -	156	4		
Gomaſtapour - -	8	5	Mahanada R.	fer.
Neemgotchy - -	12	0		
Engliſh Bazar - -	8	2		
MAULDAH - -	3	3	Ditto R.	fer.
Choudwar - -	7	2		
Egacherra - -	3	3		
Baraal - - -	5	6		
Rutwaa - -	2	6		
Ecbarpour, or Hyatpour	5	4	Nullah	ford
Biſſuntpour Gola -	11	3		
Nabobgunge - -	7	0		
	231	6		

Names of Places.	distances in Miles and Furl.		Rivers and Nullahs to be crossed.	ford or ferry.
(Purneah continued) -	231	6		
Serineah - -	8	5		
Jagrenautpour - -	12	0		
PURNEAH - -	11	0		
	263	3		
RADANAGUR. See Chandercoona - -	50	6		
RAHNY in Malduar				
Meerjaserra, in Mahrajegunge road - -	226	2		
Bydel - - -	7	5		
Cukeramony - -	6	0		
Bahmor - -	8	0		
Callyagunge - -	2	6		
Suncowr - -	6	0		
Rabny - - -	2	5		
	259	2		
RAJABARY. See Islamabad - - -	179	5		
RAJANAGUR				
Nunkissergunge, in Mulfutgunge road -	169	3		
Rajanagur - -	5	4	Calligonga	fer.
	174	7		
RAJEGUNGE, or Dinagepour. See Dellamcotta	233	1		

Names of Places.	distances in Miles and Furl.		Rivers and Nullahs to be crossed.	ford or ferry.
RAJEMAL. See Patna 1st road - - -	190	7		
RAMGUR. See Koondah road - - -	221	3		
RANGAMATTY				
1st road, by Nattore. See Bisnee - -	315	3		
2d road by Rungpour				
RUNGPOUR - -	260	5		
Cowanya - -	9	0	Monaash N.	ford
Pongah - -	9	2	Teesta N.	ford
Nawassy - -	9	3	Durla & Neelcomer Rs.	fers.
Paradanga - -	3	6	Nullah	ford
Poonkur - -	10	2	Sunecoss R.	fer.
RANGAMATTY, as before	25	2		
	327	4		
RAYMGUNGE, or Saibgunge Cantonments. See Dellamcotta -	283	6		
ROGONAUTPOUR. See Koondah - -	143	3		
ROONAY. See Chackia 2d road - - -	195	0		
ROTAS GUR				
Tickarry, in Benares 3d road - - -	329	6		

Names of Places.	distances in Miles and Furl.		Rivers and Nullahs to be crossed.	ford or ferry.
(Rotas Gur continued)	329	6		
Couch - - -	4	6		
Atee - - -	6	5		
Pogah - - -	6	0		
Badour - - -	6	0		
Norungah - -	10	2		
Byrapour - -	3	5		
Parah - - -	3	7		
Cotumbah - -	6	3		
Ramnagur - -	7	6		
Dongwar - -	8	4		
ROTAS GUR - -	8	0	Soane R.	ford
	401	4		
ROTA, or Ratta Paſs. See Monghir 3d road -	233	4		
ROYPOUR				
Kiſtnagur, in Junoh road	81	1		
Cheingſoley Chokey -	7	4	Selai R.	ford
Sunſabuddea Patterpurra	4	5		
Burra Seringa - -	6	3		
Roypour - -	5	2		
	104	7		
RUNGPOUR 1ſt road, by Buddaul				
Mootyjyl (MOORSHEDABAD) - - -	118	5		
Cuttorah - -	2	0		
Seetarampare - -	3	6	Nullah	fer.
Titalya - -	3	2	Ditto	fer.
Murcha - - -	9	2	Ditto	ford
Codalcotty Gaut - -	1	6		
	138	5		

Names of Places.	distances in Miles and Furl.		Rivers and Nullahs to be crossed.	ford or ferry.
(Rungpour continued)	138	5		
Nabobgunge - -	2	4	Ganges R.	fer.
Bauleah - - -	2	6		
Nohuttah - -	7	5		
Mootyhar Ferry -	6	2	Barruly R.	fer.
Bowanigunge - -	9	6	Nullah	fer.
Bandicurra - -	8	0	Attri R.	fer.
Merjapour haut - -	2	5	Nullah	fer.
Nagong - - -	7	4		
Saapour haut - -	6	0		
Buddlegoſſy - -	6	2		
Saumgunge - -	4	6		
Buddaul - - -	4	4	Ditto	ford
Seeallahaut - -	8	0		
Buxigunge - -	7	2	Jubuna N.	ford
Nabobgunge - -	13	0	Nullah	ford
Cooſugary - -	6	6	2 ditto	fors.
Mullung - -	11	4		
RUNGPOUR - -	7	0	Goggot R.	fer.
	260	5		
RUNGPOUR 2d road by Goragot				
Bowanigunge, as before	167	4		
Belluah Gaut - -	9	5	Goor R.	fer.
Burpookarya - -	6	7		
Carree - - -	7	1		
Banniadiggy - -	6	2		
Nandyol - -	21	0		
GORAGOT - -	14	0	Currattya R.	fer.
Haatybundar - -	11	4	Ankera N.	ford
Burradirga - -	9	4		
Mettypookre - -	4	5		
Dumdumma - -	6	3		
RUNGPOUR - - -	3	3	Goggot R.	fer.
	267	6		

Names of Places.	distances in Miles	and Furl.	Rivers and Nullahs to be crossed.	ford or ferry.
RUTTUNGUNGE				
Nulluah, in Jaffiergunge road - - -	125	2		
Behrpour - -	8	0		
Bailgutchy - -	9	4		
Nazagunge - -	3	4	Ganges R.	fer.
Ruttungunge - -	8	4		
	154	6		
RYCOTTY				
Rynabad, in Backergunge 1st road - -	115	6		
Haholly - -	6	3		
* *Rycotty* - - -	16	0	Ballasore R. & 2 Nullahs	fers.
	138	1		
RYNABAD. See Backergunge 1st road -	115	6		
SAIBGUNGE, or Raymgunge Cantonments. See Dellamcotta - -	283	6		
SANASHYGOTTA				
DINAGEPOUR, in Dellamcotta road -	233	1		
Rannygunge - -	5	1	Purnabubah R.	fer.
Singong - -	5	4	3 Nullahs	fors
Little Roopgunge -	7	3	3 ditto	fors
Dahnah - -	8	0		
Gubinagur - -	7	5	Tangan N.	fors
Tarraberry - -	5	0	Ditto	ford
Rannygunge - -	7	0		
	278	6		

Names of Places.	distances in Miles and Furl.		Rivers and Nullahs to be crossed.	ford or ferry.
(Sanashygotta continued)	278	6		
Jillee - - -	5	0		
Jivicotta - -	10	0	Tangan N.	ford
Borabery - -	5	4		
Sanashygotta - -	10	0	Dunk N.	ford
	309	2		
SANTIPOUR				
Inchura, in Patna 1st road	42	2		
Gocalgunge - -	5	0		
Santipour - -	2	6	Hoogly R.	fer.
	50	0		
SARHAUT. See Patna 2d road - - -	171	3		
SASARAM. See Benares 2d road - -	494	5		
2d road. See ditto 3d road	389	2		
SEEBGUNGE. See Bisnee	205	5		
SEEDLY Fort				
Barriapour, in Bettyah 2d road - - -	339	7		
Roussarah - -	5	6		
Manscoly - -	6	0		
Mansarah - -	9	1		
Badapour - -	8	5		
DURBUNGAH -	6	6	Buckya R.	ford
Dadail - - -	10	6		
Dundapour - -	8	4		
Piperoon - -	15	0		
Janickpour - -	11	0		
✣ Entrance of the Hills -	24	0		
✣ *Seedly* - - -	24	0		
	469	3		

Names of Places.	distances in Miles and Furl.		Rivers and Nullahs to be crossed.	ford or ferry.
SEERPOUR, in Mahmanshy, 1st road. See Dewangunge 2d road	193	4		
2d road, by Hurryal				
Runnagaut, in Kishenagur road - - -	47	4		
Naranpour - -	7	1	Nullah	fer.
Sibnybas - - -	15	2		
Corolgotchy - -	9	0		
Damorda - -	9	2	Issamutty R.	ford
Comelapour - -	10	5	Nowgonga R.	ford
Buxipour - -	10	0		
Aulumpour - -	9	2	Comer N.	ford
Custee - - -	9	6		
Pubna Nazirpour -	10	0	Ganges R.	fer.
Syngpine - -	10	6		
Chatmol - -	9	4	Attri R.	ford
Hurryal - -	10	0	Goor R.	fer.
Nowgong - -	3	0		
Tarwas - -	6	1		
Bowanypour - -	10	0		
Seerpour - -	8	2		
	195	3		
SEERPOUR (Jillee)				
Jummucandy - -	108	6		
Muyser - -	3	4	More R.	ford
Curgong - -	3	2		
Seerpour - - -	7	2		
	122	6		
SERAMPOUR, in Bahar. See Patna 3d road	191	5		

Names of Places.	diſtances in Miles and Furl.		Rivers and Nullahs to be croſſed.	ford or ferry.
SERAMPOUR (Daniſh Factory)				
Solkee - - -	1	6	Hoogly R.	fer.
Bally Creek - -	4	1	- -	fer.
Serampour - -	7	0		
	12	7		
SERRIS				
Daoudnagur, in Benares 3d road - - -	362	0		
Piprah Gur - -	11	0		
Serris - - -	10	0		
	383	0		
SEWAN, or Alligunge				
Moneah, in Benares 1ſt road	421	4		
Cheeran - -	6	7	Ganges R.	fer.
CHUPRAH - -	7	6		
Jaitpour - -	13	3		
Bagorah - -	11	3		
Huſſar - - -	5	6		
Sewan - - -	7	2		
	473	7		
SHEERGOTTY				
Gayah, in Benares 3d road - -	314	4		
Buttee - - -	6	6		
Colera - - -	5	0		
Gorua - - -	6	6		
Sheergotty - -	10	0		
	343	0		
SHILBERIS. See Buggora - - -	200	1		

Names of Places.	diſtances in Miles and Furl.		Rivers and Nullahs to be croſſed.	ford or ferry.
SIBNYBAS. See Seerpour 2d road - -	69	7		
SICLYGULLY. See Patna 1ſt Road - -	210	2		
SILHET				
DACCA - -	179	5		
Molapara - -	9	7	Balloo C. & Luckya R.	fers.
Ballya - -	2	3		
Saatgong - -	6	6		
Nurſingdee - -	7	2	Megna R.	fer.
Corallya - -	9	5	Little Megna R.	fer.
Novenagur - -	7	0	Teetas R.	fer.
Guſipour - -	5	2	Ditto	fer.
Suneram pour - -	8	0		
Cutchua haut - -	13	6	Bemalya R.	ford
Lacki - - -	11	0	Kohi R.	ford
Sujatpour - -	7	6	Brack R.	fer.
Banniachung - -	12	1		
Connipour - -	9	4		
Agna - - -	5	2	Nullah	ford
Cattaya - - -	11	0		
Bunbaug - -	10	0	Buſſya N.	ford
SILHET - -	9	2	Soorma R.	fer.
	325	3		
SILLEE. See Junoh Paſs	204	3		
SILLEEGORY				
Sanaſbygotta - -	309	2		
Silleegory - -	6	6		
	316	0		

Names of Places.	distances in Miles	and Furl.	Rivers and Nullahs to be crossed.	ford or ferry.
SINGBOOM 1st road, by Coppraguddy Pass				
MIDNAPOUR - -	74	4		
Mohdypour - -	7	6	Cassai R.	ford
Jinjenny - -	6	6		
Boitau - - -	7	2	Ditto twice	fors.
Pertapour - -	6	0		
Candareeah - -	6	4		
Allumpour - -	6	7		
Beend - - -	8	0	Dolong R.	ford
Deresеah - -	10	2		
Narsingur - -	9	1		
Gatseela - -	6	2		
Moleeah - -	8	4		
Subunreka R. -	2	7	- -	ford
Copraguddy Pass -	4	3		
Calcapour - -	2	5		
Patacka - -	6	1	2 Nullahs	fors.
Huldypcokre - -	4	2		
SINGBOOM, by report	40	0		
	218	0		
SINGBOOM 2d road, by Notagur Pass				
Narsingur, as before	143	0		
Notagur Pass -	5	4	Subunreka R.	ford
Kerbony - -	11	4		
Coontah - - -	11	0		
Huldypookre - -	15	0		
SINGBOOM - -	40	0		
	226	0		
SINGBOOM 3d road, by Doarsinnee Pass				
Janpour, in Soojanhy Pass road - - -	103	7		
Gopalnapour - -	4	4	Subunreka R.	ford
	108	3		

Names of Places.	distances in Miles and Furl.		Rivers and Nullahs to be crossed.	ford or ferry.
(Singboom 3d road continued) - -	108	3		
Saseelah - -	8	6		
Pauraw - - -	8	0		
Juncaw - - -	13	4		
Tooluck - -	18	0	Doarsinnee defile	
Asnaha - - -	5	0		
Guidee Gaut - -	5	0		
Ouleedy - -	1	4		
Gallegur - -	1	6		
SINGBOOM, by report	40	0		
	209	7		
SINGBOOM 4th road, by Baumeen Pass				
Juncaw, as before -	138	6		
Baumeen Pass -	5	0		
Coontah - -	16	0		
Baumeen Gaut - -	5	4	Kerki R.	ford
Gomahnee - -	6	0		
Colgee - - -	4	3		
Dallamaw - -	4	6		
Curree Pass - -	1	2		
SINGBOOM, by report	40	0		
	221	5		
SINGHYA. See Bettyah 1st road - - -	417	6		
SOOJANHY Pass, in Mohrbunge				
MIDNAPOUR - -	74	4		
Mohdypour - -	7	6	Cassai R.	ford
Saumnagur - -	13	2		
	95	4		

Names of Places.	distances in Miles and Furl.		Rivers and Nullahs to be crossed.	ford or ferry.
(Soojanhy Pass continued)	95	4		
Janpour - - -	8	2		
Dumarear - -	7	4	Subunreka R.	ford
Dinnamary - -	8	6	Nullah	ford
Burpudda - -	12	0		
HARRIERPOUR -	9	0		
Coontah - -	9	6		
Balbudderpour -	10	4		
Gurredur - -	10	4		
Cuttipara - -	6	7		
Soojanhy Pass -	4	0		
	182	5		
SOOPOUR. See Soory	92	6		
SOORY, or Hyderabad 1st road. See Nagore	118	5		
2d road, by Soopour				
BURDWAN, in Patna 2d road - - -	61	4		
Allumpour - -	6	4		
Oregong - -	8	4	Curree N.	ford
Gubindpour - -	6	6	Cunoor N.	ford
Soopour - - -	9	4	Adji R.	ford
Surrool - - -	3	1		
Saturya - -	4	3		
Gurgarya - -	6	3		
Purunderpour -	3	5	Baccasore N.	ford
Soory - - -	5	1		
	115	3		
SOOTY 1st road. See Patna 1st road - -	153	6		

Names of Places.	distances in Miles and Furl.		Rivers and Nullahs to be crossed.	ford or ferry.
SOOTY 2d road				
Mootyjyl (MOORSHEDABAD)	118	5		
Moradbaug - -	4	0	Cossimbuzar R.	fer.
BERNAGUR - -	4	0		
Ghysabad - -	3	0		
Gadee - - -	7	0		
Churkah - -	6	6		
Belgotta - -	2	4	Bansli N.	fer.
Gareeah field - -	5	2		
Sooty - - -	3	6		
	154	7		
SUAGRA				
CHUPRAH, in Sewan road	436	1		
Gudena - - -	5	2		
Manjee - - -	6	2		
Taujepour - -	6	7		
Teswan - - -	6	6		
Nurhun - - -	9	4		
Durowly - -	10	0		
Gutini - - -	8	0		
Suegra - - -	5	0		
	493	6		
SUJATPOUR. See Silhet	268	2		
SULTANABAD, or Birkooty. See Patchwarry	149	3		
SUMMUTGUR. See Patna 1st road - -	59	7		

Names of Places.	diſtances in Miles and Furl.		Rivers and Nullahs to be croſſed.	ford or ferry.
SUNAMOOKY Aurung				
Indoſs - - -	71	2		
Kiſtnagur - -	8	0		
Donſemalee - -	6	3		
Sunamooky - -	6	0		
	91	5		
SUNERAMPOUR. See Silhet - -	248	6		
SURDA. See Biſnee -	137	1		
SURROOL Aurung. See Soory 2d road -	95	7		
SURROOPOUR Purgannah				
DINAGEPOUR in Dellamcotta road - -	233	1		
Bagduar Gaut -	8	6	- -	2 fers
Comergunge - -	10	3		
Samgunge Cutchery -	10	0		
	262	2		
SURYA, or Suramma. See Patna 2d road -	183	1		
SUSUNG Purgannah				
Hajygunge, in Dacca Road	139	2		
Diagunge - -	3	0	Ganges R. & a Nullah	fer.
Jattrapour - -	9	2	Iſſamutty R.	ford
	151	5		

Names of Places.	distances in Miles and Furl.		Rivers and Nullahs to be crossed.	ford or ferry.
(Susung Purgunnah, continued	151	5		
Gwalparah - -	12	0		
Baubunpara - -	11	2	Dollascry R.	fer.
Attyah - -	8	6	2 Nullahs	ford
Batcoorah - -	6	5		
Buketa Aurung -	3	4		
Hummidpour - -	8	0		
Chamtarra - -	6	2		
Moodupour - -	10	1	Bunse R.	ford
Ramchunpour -	17	4	Nullah	ford
Bygonbarry - -	11	4	2 ditto	fors.
Purangunge - -	1	2	Burrampooter R.	fer.
Teetpour - -	5	0	Nullah	ford
Niatty - - -	6	4		
Okyle - - -	5	5		
Bowhaaly - -	8	0		
Cungas River - -	6	2		
Noparrah - -	6	2		
Duregapour Cutchery -	3	6		
	289	6		
SUTALURY, 1st road. See Backergunge 1st road	150	5		
2d road				
Madapassa in Backergunge, 2d road - -	184	7		
Mogassy - - -	7	4	2 Nullahs	ford
Sutalury - - -	5	0		
	197	3		
TAMLOOK				
Baugnan in Midnapour, 2d road - -	29	5		

Names of Places.	diſtances in Miles and Furl.		Rivers and Nullahs to be croſſed.	ford or ferry.
(Tamlook continued) -	29	5		
Bynapour - -	5	0		
Tamlook - -	9	0	Roopnaran & a Nullah	fers.
	43	5		
TARRAPOUR, 1ſt road. See Monghir, 2d road	255	2		
2d road. See Curruckpour, 2d road	286	5		
TAUJEPOUR. See Mahrajegunge - -	253	7		
TEETBADDY Aurung Perralya, in Laour road	207	7		
Teetbaddy - -	9	4		
	217	3		
TERRIAGULLY. See Patna, 1ſt road -	223	0		
TICKARRY. See Benares 3d road - -	329	6		
TIPERAH. See Kundal	227	4		
TOMAR, or Tamar				
Patcom - -	183	6		
* *Tomar* - - -	15	0		
	198	6		

Names of Places.	distances in Miles and Furl.		Rivers and Nullahs to be crossed.	ford or ferry.
TOONRY. See Patna, 3d road - - -	177	5		
TOREE				
Tikoo, in Palamow road	288	7		
Tikoo Paſs - -	3	6		
Toree - - -	9	2		
	301	7		
TORROFF. See Bangah	278	0		
TUREE, or Tuer				
Sarhaut, in Patna 2d road	171	3		
Luckorceah - -	8	4		
Mudwun - -	3	6		
Bankah - -	4	5		
Turee - - -	4	6		
	193	0		
TURKI. See Bettyah 2d road - - -	413	4		

ISLAMA-

ISLAMABAD CORRECTED.

Meerjapour (page 37)	263	1		
Fenny R. West Side -	3	0		
49 Milestone -	1	6	Fenny	fer.
Jurilgunge - -	4	2		
Meercaserai (Bungaloe)	6	6		
Comildar - -	7	0		
Seetacoon (Bungaloe)	5	4		
Cumarya Bridge -	8	0		
Cuddumrusil (Bungaloe)	5	4		
Jaffierabad (Bungaloe)	5	6		
ISLAMABAD (Old Fort)	6	2		
	316	7		

TABLES OF ROADS,

FROM

MOORSHEDABAD OR MOOTYJYL,

TO ALL THE PRINCIPAL PLACES IN

BENGAL AND BAHAR.

Expreſſing the Length of the Stages, and the Number and Situation of the Fords and Ferries.

TABLES OF ROADS,

From MOORSHEDABAD or MOOTYJYL, to all the principal Places in BENGAL and BAHAR.

Names of Places.	distances in Miles and Furl.		Rivers and Nullahs to be crossed.	ford or ferry.
AHMIRABADS Purgannah				
Chandergunge, in Islamabad road - -	232	6		
Buzra Cutcherry -	6	2		
	239	0		
AMBOOAH. See Calcutta, 1st road - - -	69	5		
AMMERPOUR, in Morung				
PURNEAH - -	144	6		
AMMERPOUR (page 1)	75	7		
	220	5		
ARRAH. See Benares, 1st road - - -	319	5		
ATTYAH. See Pucculoe	128	1		
AUGURDEEP. See Calcutta 1st road -	40	3		

AWMORE Purgannah				
Sonkoe, in Monghyr, 3d road - - -	21	2		
Pyker - - -	13	0		
Noangong - -	5	0	Banſli R.	ford
Puccoree Cutcherry -	10	4		
	49	6		
AYTURAH. See Burwah	101	7		
AZMERIGUNGE. See Silhet - - -	236	7		
BACKERGUNGE				
Balloo - - -	5	5	Nullah	fer.
Dultabazar - -	2	5		
Azimgunge - -	11	6		
Culcully Termony -	8	2	Jellinghy R.	ford
Hurryſongkor - -	11	4		
Damadure - -	10	4		
Cuſtee - - -	11	0		
Comercally - -	10	4	Gorroy R.	ford
Soripour - - -	4	6		
Moddapour (Pangſa)	8	2		
Sanaparah - -	10	0		
Behrpour - -	4	1	Chundnah R.	fer.
Nolluah - - -	8	0		
Booſnah - -	6	3	Comer N.	ford
Jaynagur - -	5	7		
Callinagur - -	10	2		
Muxoodpour -	5	1		
Batcamara - -	8	4		
Dignagur - -	4	6		
Hobibgunge - -	11	0	Comer N.	ford
Kalkenny - -	9	6	Ditto	ford
Gurnady - -	12	0		
Idrackpour - -	5	6	Nullah	fer.
Madapaſſa - -	12	6	3 ditto	fer.
	199	0		

(Backergunge continued)	199	0		
Gurypaſſa - -	8	6	3 Nullahs	fer.
Backergunge - -	7	4	1 ditto	fer.
	215	2		
BAHAR 1ſt road. See Patna				
2d road - -	236	4		
2d road by Monghyr				
Rampour, in Patna 1ſt road - - -	207	4		
BAHAR (page 6) -	44	0		
	251	4		
BALASORE. See Ganjam	226	3		
BALLITUNGHY. See Putimahry - -	28	2		
BALGUDA. See Bahar 2d road - - -	212	6		
BAR. See Patna, 1ſt road	244	0		
BAULEAH. See Rungpour, 1ſt road -	25	2		
BAUMEEN Paſs, in Moherbunge				
Juncaw, in Doarſinny Road	210	1		
Baumeen Paſs - -	5	0		
	215	1		
BELCUCHY. See Puccaloe	105	2		

BENARES, 1st road by Buxar				
PATNA (page 55) -	281	5		
Buxar (page 8) -	85	1		
	366	6		
BENARES, 2d road by Birboom, Gayah, and Saseram				
Islamnagur in Patna 2d road - - -	202	4		
Rypoor - - -	12	0		
Curree - - -	6	4		
Bertha, or Burdoo -	6	6		
BENARES (page 9) -	189	0		
	416	6		
BENARES 3d road, by Mawbellipour				
PATNA (page 54) -	281	5		
BENARES (page 8) -	165	4		
	447	1		
BEERCOOL				
Narangur, in Ganjam road	165	3		
Mackoorya - -	5	6	Cullyaghi N.	fer.
Syburrah - -	7	0	Nullah	
Nanjoorah - -	5	0		
Moradabad - -	3	2		
Lungrye - - -	5	0		
Pundooah - -	5	2		
Meergooda - -	5	0		
Beercool - - -	4	0		
Beercool (Bungaloe) -	3	1		
	208	6		
BERNAGUR, in Raujeshy See Sooty 2d road -	8	0		

BERNAGUR, in Purneah				
PURNEAH - -	144	6		
Old Coosy R. - -	5	2	- -	ford
Ecteeapour - -	8	0		
Coondwa Gaut -	3	2		
Bernagur - -	13	0	Coosy, or Cosa R.	fer.
	174	2		
BETTYAH, 1st road by Patna				
PATNA (page 55) -	281	5		
BETTYAH (page 10)	100	0		
	381	5		
BETTYAH, 2d road by Turki				
MONGHYR, in Patna 1st road - - -	182	1		
BETTYAH (page 11)	178	1		
	360	2		
BEYHAR, or Coos Beyhar. See Buxaduar - -	193	5		
BEJURAH				
Hurringber, in Torroff road	238	3		
Bejurah - -	5	0		
	243	3		
BIRBOOM, or Nagore. See Patna, 2d road -	70	5		
BIRKOOTY				
Baderpour, in Monghyr 3d road - - -	35	2		
Birkooty - -	3	6		
	39	0		

BISNEE				
RUNGPOUR - -	142	0		
Cowanya - -	9	0	Moonaafh N.	ford
Pongah - - -	9	2	Teefta N.	ford
Nawaffey - -	9	3	Durla & Neelcomer	fers.
Paradanga - -	3	6	Nullah	ford
Poonkur - -	10	2	Sunecofs R.	fer.
Bifnee (page 12) - -	97	2		
	280	7		
BISSUNPOUR. See Huldipookre - -	113	4		
BITTREBUND Purganah (*Paradangah* Cutchery) fee Bifnee - -	173	7		
BOGLIPOUR. See Patna 1ft road - -	144	3		
BOGARYA. See Monghyr 2d and 3d roads	167	5		
BOGWANGOLA				
Cuttorah - -	2	0		
Palafbery - -	5	1	Nullah	ford
Baderpour - -	4	3		
Bogwangola - -	5	0	Culcully N.	ford
	16	4		
BOOSNAH. See Backergunge - - -	113	2		

BOWANIPOUR. (in Purneah) - - -				
Caragola, in Purneah 2d road - - -	119	3		
Chandpour Gaut -	8	4	Coosy R.	fer.
Ghiddara - -	2	4		
Bowanipour - -	9	2		
	139	5		
BOWANIGUNGE. See Rungpour, 1st road	48	7		
BUDDAUL. See Rungpour, 1st road -	88	4		
BUDGEBUDGE				
CALCUTTA - -	118	5		
Surman's Bridge -	2	7		
Budgebudge - -	10	5	2 Nullahs	
	132	1		
BUGGURA (Cutchery of Shilberis)				
Carree in Rungpour, 2d road - - -	72	4		
Ghiabunder - -	7	1	Nagore N.	ford
Buggura - - -	14	0		
	93	5		
BULRAMPOUR. See Huldypookre - -	158	5		
BURDWAN, 1st road by Cutwa. See Ganjam	73	7		
2d road by Jummucandy				
COSSIMBUZAR - -	2	3	Cossimbuzar R.	2 fers

(Burdwan continued) -	2	3		
Moketerpour Choky -	6	0	Nullah	ford
Cuſbaſpour - -	8	2		
Jummucandy - -	5	6	More R.	ford
Aſſoah - - -	6	1		
Tarrapour - -	3	7	Queyah R.	fer.
Rye - - -	9	2		
Mongulcote - -	12	3	Adji R.	ford
Arrawah - -	4	6		
Maſſundy - -	7	7	Curree N.	ford
BURDWAN - -	8	0		
	74	5		

BURRABOOM				
Muccroo, in Singboom road - - -	170	7		
Burraboom - -	3	6		
	174	5		

BURHAMPOUR Cantonments				
COSSIMBUZAR -	2	3	Coſſimbuzar R.	2 fers
Burhampour - -	3	0		
	5	3		

BURWAH				
Soory, in Patna 2d road	54	5		
Kiſtnagur - -	11	5		
Dubrajepour - -	3	1		
Lacaracoonda - -	8	6		
Luckanpour - -	6	7		
Jamgong - -	9	4	Adji R.	ford
Aytura - - -	7	3		
Dummoodah R. -	7	0	- -	ford
PACHETE - -	8	7		
ROGONAUTPORE	8	1		
Purſeah - -	14	0		
Byra - - -	4	7	Guy N.	ford
Jubbrah - -	9	0		
Naranpour - -	8	5		
	162	3		

(Burwah continued) -	162	3		
Radnagur - -	5	2		
Cosmar - - -	10	1		
Petrabad - -	5	5		
Burwah (page 16) -	135	1		
	318	4		
BURGANCOOTY				
Gobingunge, in Rungpour road - - -	106	3		
Burgancooty - -	2	0		
	108	3		
BURRUTPOUR, in Futtysing				
Jummucandy, in Burdwan 2d road - -	22	3		
Burrutpour - -	6	5	Queah R.	fer.
	29	0		
BUXAR. See Benares 1st road - - -	366	6		
BUXIGUNGE. See Rungpour, 1st road -	103	6		
BUXIPOUR, in Mahmudshi. See Jessore Culna	65	3		
BUXADUAR				
RUNGPOUR (page 63)	142	0		
Buxaduar (page 16) -	95	0		
	237	0		

BYKONTPOUR, in Buttishazary				
Saibgunge, or *Rayngunge*, in Dellamcotta road -	165	1		
Bykontpour (page 17) -	36	1		
	201	2		
BYGONBARY. See Silhet 1st road - -	160	1		
CALCUTTA, 1st road				
COSSIMBUZAR -	2	3	Cossimbuzar R.	2 fer.
Chunapour - -	2	7		
Burruah - -	10	4		
Daudpour - -	3	7		
Plassey - - -	6	4		
Augurdeep - -	14	2		
Battolee - -	3	0	Ditto R.	ford
Jahanagur - -	11	1		
Summutgur - -	4	2		
Mirzapour - -	4	1	Curree N.	fer.
Culna - - -	4	0		
Ambooah - -	2	6		
Inchurah - -	6	6		
Niaserai - -	8	7		
Bansbaria - -	4	4	2 Nullahs	fers
HOOGLY - -	3	2		
Chandernagore - -	4	3		
Ghyretty Cantonments -	4	3		
Sooksor - - - -	7	1	Hoogly R. & a Nullah	fer.
Barnagur - -	4	7		
CALCUTTA Old Fort	4	7		
	118	5		
CALCUTTA, 2d road by Kishenagur				
Plassey, as before -	26	1		
Pangotta - -	5	6	Nullah	fer.
	31	7		

(Calcutta continued)	31	7		
Bickrampour - -	7	0		
Jugdanpour - -	3	6		
Niahaut - - -	7	7		
Gwabree - -	7	2	Jellinghy R.	ford
KISHENAGUR -	2	0		
Taxal Ferry - -	8	6	Nullah	fer.
Barrasat - - -	3	1		
Runnagaut - -	7	3	Nullah	ford
Chandpour - -	5	4	2 ditto	1 for. 1 fer.
Hell, or Burrye -	7	5		
Jagoleah - -	4	4	Jubuna N.	ford
Amedunga - -	9	1		
Barraset - -	7	2	Nullah	ford
Dumdum - -	7	4		
CALCUTTA - -	6	0		
	126	4		
CANTALBARY, in Bootan. See Luckiduar	196	2		
CARAGOLA. See Purneah, 2d road	119	3		
CAULEAH. See Pucculoe	101	1		
CAUGMAHRY				
Potul, in Pucculoe road	113	1		
Caugmahry - -	9	4		
	122	5		
CHANDERNAGORE. See Calcutta, 1st road	97	3		

CHANDERCONA				
Jacrah, in Ganjam road	117	7		
Chandercona - -	4	6		
	122	5		
CHANDPOUR. See Iſlamabad - -	189	7		
CHACKI, or Fort Haſtings, 1ſt road. See Patna 2d road - - -	155	0		
2d road. Surya in Patna, 2d road -	122	6		
Roonay - - -	12	1		
Ponaſſey - - -	8	0		
Chacki - - -	9	2		
	152	1		
CHATNA. See Singboom	121	5		
CHATMOL				
Bauleah, in Rungpour, 1ſt road	25	2		
Surdah - - -	12	2		
Hazeryhutty - -	4	0	Nullah	ford
Pokareeah - -	5	5		
Battorya - -	8	6		
Burkagaſſy - -	11	0		
Marmee - - -	2	0		
Autlanka - -	9	4	Attri R.	fer.
Chatmol - - -	5	4		
	83	7		
CHILMARY				
Gobigunge, in Rungpour 3d road - -	106	3		
Motrah - - -	4	3	Nulluah N.	ford
	110	6		

(Chilmary continued)	110	6		
Noongola - -	9	4	Goggot R.	fer.
Boggurya - -	7	0	Coolny R.	fer.
Nallagunge - -	8	0	Serri R.	fer.
Chilmary - -	7	1	Teesta N.	ford
	142	3		
CHINSURA				
HOOGLY, in Calcutta 1st road - - -	93	0		
Chinsura - - -	1	6		
	94	6		
CHICHACOTTA. See Buxaduar - -	212	1		
CHITTAGONG. See Islamabad - - -	315	1		
CHOGONG. See Dewangunge 2d road -	69	6		
CHOWTAH, in Futtypour				
Curoondah, in Soopour road - - -	36	6		
Chowtah - - -	9	6		
	46	4		
CHOWSAR				
Buxar, in Benares 1st road	366	6		
Chowsar - -	6	6	Nullah	fer.
	373	4		
CHUPRAH. See Sewaan	317	4		

CHUNARGUR				
Mogulserai, in Benares 2d road - - -	408	0		
CHUNARGUR -	18	0		
	426	0		
COLINDA. See Islamabad	247	5		
COLGONG. See Patna 1st road - - -	124	7		
COMILLAH, or Tiperah				
DACCA - -	164	7		
Futtulah - -	6	5	2 Nullahs	fer.
Naraingunge - -	2	6		
Goojaleah - -	7	2	- -	3fer.
Allynya - -	9	0	Megna R. & 2 N.	fer.
Daoudcandy - -	0	6		
COMILLAH (page 42)	32	7		
	224	1		
COMERCALLY. See Backergunge - -	71	6		
CONSUMAGUNGE. See Dellamcotta -	137	0		
CONCHON. See Dinagepour 2d road -	76	0		
COORSAH - -				
Saftibary, in Buxaduar road	155	7		
Quoilagot - -	6	3	Durla R.	fer.
Coorsah - -	6	6	Neelcomer R.	fer.
	169	0		

COOSERA. See Bahar 2d road - - -	236	0		
COPRAGUDDY Pafs. See Huldipookre - -	221	5		
COSSIMBUZAR -	2	3	Coffimbuzar R.	2 fer.
COTWALLY				
Englifh Bazar, in Purneah road - - -	66	6		
Cotwally - -	5	4		
	72	2		
CULNA, in Burdwan. See Calcutta 1ft road -	66	7		
CULNA, in Jeffore				
Hurrifongkor, in Backergunge road - -	39	6		
Goalgom - -	9	7		
Boladinga - -	6	0		
Buxipour - -	9	6	Comer N.	ford
Orinacoora - -	10	2	Nullah	ford
Jennidah - -	11	7	Nowgonga R.	ford
NULDINGAH -	8	2	Sittaryah R.	ford
Nazumpour - -	9	4		
Arroporah - -	6	5		
MOORLEY, or *JESSORE*	4	3	Boirub R.	fer.
Chandoly - -	8	0		
Ecterpour - -	7	0		
Samgunge - -	8	6		
Collifpour - -	6	0		
Culna - - -	2	4	Ditto	fer.
	148	4		

CURGONG				
Cuſhaſpour, in Burdwan 2d road - -	16	5		
Curgong - - -	8	3		
	25	0		
CURRUCKPOUR, 1ſt road by Terriagully				
Pialapour in Patna, 1ſt road	113	3		
CURRUCKPOUR (p. 22)	62	1		
	175	4		
2d road by Deogur. See Monghir 2d road - -	202	0		
CURRUCKDEAH 1ſt road. See Patna 3d road -	172	0		
2d road				
Aytura, in Burwah road	101	7		
Curruckdeah (p. 58) -	76	2		
	178	1		
CURRYBARY Purgannah. It lies on the eaſt ſide of the Burrampooter river, oppoſite to Chilmary.				
CURYGONG				
Noongola in Chilmary road	120	2		
Barrabuldya - -	8	4	Coolny R.	fer.
Panſgutchy - -	8	0	Moonaaſh N.	2 fors
Olyapour - -	11	0	Teeſta N.	fer.
Duregapour - -	5	4	Bamaany N.	ford
Curygong - - -	8	2		
	161	4		
CUTSEE. See Backergunge	61	2		

CUTTUPGUNGE. The same as Mahrajegunge	159	2		
CUTTAC. See Ganjam	332	7		
CUTWA. See Ganjam	38	5		
DACCA, 1st road				
Hurrysongkor, in Backergunge road - -	39	6		
Damadure - -	10	4		
Shawpour - -	3	6		
Comitpour - -	5	6	Ganges R.	fer.
Pubna - - -	6	2		
Sujanagur - -	12	0	Arti R.	fer.
Nazagunge - -	12	4		
Ruttungunge - -	8	4		
Jaffiergunge - -	10	0	2 Rivers	fers
Chanpara - -	6	3		
Jeetka - - -	6	7	Cantabotey R.	fer.
Jattrapour - -	5	2	Surramutty R.	ford
Burruacally - -	8	0		
Bandura - -	3	1	Issamutty R.	fer.
Churan - - -	9	2		
Seckinagur - -	2	4	2 Nullahs	fer.
Pattergotta - -	8	4	Nullah	fer.
DACCA - -	6	0	Issamutty & Boorigonga	fer.
	164	7		
DACCA, 2d road by Hajygunge				
Moddapour, in Backergunge road - -	84	6		
Bailgutchy - -	7	1	Chundnah R.	fer.
	91	7		

(Dacca 2d road continued)	91	7		
Cameldiggy - -	11	1	Nullah	ford
Angordya - -	8	0		
Kishnapour - -	4	5		
Hajygunge - -	9	0		
Nurilapour - -	7	0	Ganges R.	fer.
Mynehaut - -	3	0		
Nabobgunge - -	7	2	Issamutty R.	fer.
Churan - -	6	0		
DACCA, as before	17	0		
	164	7		
DAOUDNAGUR. See Benares 2d road -	318	3		
DARRA, in Jungleterry, 1st road by Terriagully				
Pialapour, in Patna 1st road - - -	113	3		
Buddlegunge - -	3	4		
Sowlee - - -	6	0		
Mehaw, or Meyammah	12	0		
Beldeeah - -	8	4		
Simulpour - -	11	2		
Darra - - -	7	4		
	162	1		
DARRA, 2d road by Sarhaut				
Sarhaut, in Patna 2d road	111	0		
Darra (page 25) -	43	6		
	154	6		
DARRA, 3d road by Patchwarry. See Monghir 3d road - -	95	3		

DELLAMCOTTA, in Bootan				
Bomineah - -	8	3		
Dellamcotta (page 26)	220	0		
	228	3		
DEOGUR. See Patna 2d road - - -	134	4		
DEOPOUR				
Ayturah, in Burwah road	101	7		
Deopour (page 27) -	43	7		
	145	6		
DEWANGUNGE (in Patladah) 1st road				
Seebgunge, in Rungpour 3d road - - -	95	3		
Curryabadder - -	13	0	Nulua N.	ford
Burrudcally - -	9	0	Goggot R.	fer.
Dewangunge - -	12	0	2 Nullahs	fers.
	129	3		
DEWANGUNGE, 2d road by Nattore and Seerpour				
Bauleah, in Rungpour 1st road - - -	25	2		
Kopposseah - -	6	2		
Birraldo - -	6	3		
Pootyah - - -	3	3		
NATTORE - -	10	1		
Dewangunge (page 27)	89	4		
	140	7		
DEWANSERAI. See Patna 1st road - -	16	3		
DINAGEPOUR 1st road. See Dellamcotta -	114	4		

Place	Miles	Furlongs	River	Ferry
DINAGEPOUR, 2d road by Sumdeah				
Nohutta in Rungpour 1ſt road - - -	32	7		
Goſah - - -	9	7	Barruly R.	fer.
Doolabarry - -	9	6		
Limbobarya - -	8	0		
Maddapour - -	7	4	Attri R.	fer.
Conclon - - -	8	0		
Rangamatty - -	7	4		
Balloogaut - -	7	0		
Puttyram - - -	9	2		
Sumdeah - -	14			
DINAGEPOUR -	11	5	Attri R.	fer.
	125	3		
DOARSINNY Paſs. See Huldipookre, 3d road				
DOBAGAUT, or Mulcalgur Paſs. See Noony 2d road - -	63	1		
DOESAH. The ſame as Chuta Nagpour -				
DOOLABARRY. See Dinagepour 2d road	52	4		
DUGALHATTY				
Nogong, in Rungpour 1ſt road - - -	67	0		
Dugalhatty - -	3	0		
	70	0		
DURBUNGAH. See Seedley	257	4		

GOPAULGUNGE				
Boosnah, in Backergunge road - - -	113	2		
MAHMUDPOUR -	8	6	Burrashee R.	fer.
Bolassey - - - -	9	4	2 Nullahs	ford
Kolna - - -	8	4	Nowgonga R.	fer.
Cajoll - - -	9	6	- -	2 fer.
Dungree - -	3	0	- -	fer.
Gopaulgunge - -	4	6	- -	2 fer.
	157	4		
GOMASTAPOUR. See Purneah 1st road -	46	4		
GORAGOT. See Rungpour 3d road - -	113	6		
GOTTAUL. Utcharlon in Ganjam road -	88	3		
Jahanabad - -	12	6		
Dewangunge - -	5	6	Dalkisor R.	fer.
Gottaul - - -	10	4	2 Nullahs	fer.
	117	3		
GOUR Ruins				
Nabobgunge in Dellamcotta road - - -	32	2		
Seebgunge - -	11	0	Mahanada R.	fer.
Pookarya - -	4	6		
Habasconna Gaut, in *Gour*	11	2		
	59	3		
GOWGATCHY				
HOOGLY in Calcutta 1st road - -	93	0		
Batpara - - -	2	5	Hoogly R.	fer.
Gowgatchy - -	4	5		
	[illegible]	[illegible]		

GUBINAGUR. See Sanashygotta - -	148	1		
GUIDORE. See Patna 2d road - - -	183	0		
GURNADY. See Backergunge - - -	180	4		
GUZGOTTA				
RUNGPOUR - -	142	0		
Guzgotta - -	7	4	2 Nullahs	fors
	149	4		
GWAHREE. See Calcutta 2d road - -	57	6		
HAJYPOUR. See Bettya 1st road - - -	286	3		
HAJYGUNGE. See Dacca 2d road - -	124	5		
HARRIERPOUR				
MIDNAPOUR in Ganjam road - - -	146	0		
HARRIERPOUR (page 71)	66	5		
	212	5		
HENDOOAH, or Herboe. See Noony - -	100	2		
HOBIBGUNGE. See Backergunge - - -	158	6		

DUTTYA Jangerpour Purganah				
Beëas, in Pecculoe road	71	1		
Bogulcman - -	9	4		
Bobanganty Cutchery -	6	4		
	87	1		
DYNAPOUR Cantonments. See Benares 1st road	293	1		
ENGLISH Bazar. See Purneah 1st road -	60	6		
FRINGYBAZAR				
DACCA - -	165	7		
Naraingunge - -	9	3	2 Nullahs	fer.
Fringybazar - -	3	1	Issamutty R.	fer.
	177	3		
GANJAM				
Plassey, in Calcutta 1st road	26	1		
Cutwa - - -	12	2	Cossimbuzar R.	ford
Ninghenserai - -	13	6		
Balkissenserai - -	10	6		
BURDWAN - -	10	6	Curree N.	ford
Mogulmary - -	12	2	Dummooda R.	ford
Utcharlon - -	2	2		
Dalkisor R. - -	6	2	- -	ford
Puccaserai - -	7	4		
Madapour - -	7	6		
Jacrah - - -	8	0		
Naradowl - -	6	0		
Assarapour - -	3	4		
Amleah - - -	5	3		
Bunpour - - -	6	0		
MIDNAPOUR -	7	2		
Carackpour - -	5	4	Cassai R.	ford
	151	2		

(Ganjam continued)	151	2		
Mutkirchoky -	5	0		
Narangur - -	8	7	Culliaghi N.	fer.
Ganjam (page 30) -	278	3		
	443	4		
GAREEAH Field. See Sooty 2d road -	32	4		
GAYAH. See Benares 2d road - - -	270	7		
GENTIAH				
SILHET - -	290	0		
Chicknacole Hills -	9	6		
Rannee-ca Tallaw -	7	6		
GENTIAH - -	7	0	Nullah	ford
	314	4		
GHYRETTY. See Calcutta 1st road -	101	6		
GOALPARA				
RAGAMATTY -	208	7		
Dudekoar - -	17	0	Sunkos R. Gourong R.	fer. ford
Jughigopa - -	21	0	Champomatty R.	fer.
Goalpara - -	5	2	Burrumpooter R.	fer.
	252	1		
GOBINGUNGE. See Rungpour 3d road - -	106	3		
GODAGARY. See Dellamcotta - -	23	6		

HOOGLY. See Calcutta 1ſt road - - -	93	0		
HULDIPOOKRE 1ſt road by Notagur Paſs				
BURDWAN in Ganjam road - - -	73	7		
Moor - - -	7	0	Dummoodah R.	ford
Dubrajehaut - -	6	4		
Indos - - -	4	1		
Balſee - - -	5	6		
Gopalnagur - -	8	5	Dalkiſor R.	ford
BISSUNPOUR - -	7	5		
Purruttumpour -	7	4		
Jambuddeah - -	9	4		
Mandaree - -	5	2	Selai R.	ford
Sunſabuddea Patterpurra	7	4		
Burra Seringa - -	6	3		
Bulrampour - -	9	0	Caſſai R.	ford
Bunpour - -	8	6		
Allumpour - -	6	2		
Bautconda - -	12	6	Dolong R.	ford
Narſingur - -	13	2		
Notagur Paſs - -	5	4	Subunreeka R.	ford
Kerbonee - -	11	4		
Coontah - -	11	0		
Huldipookre - -	15	0		
	242	5		
HULDIPOOKRE 2d road, by Copraguddy Paſs				
Narſingur as before -	199	5		
Gatſeela - -	6	4		
Molecah - - -	8	2		
Subunreeka R. - -	2	7	- -	ford
Copraguddy Paſs -	4	3		
Calcapour - -	2	5		
Huldipookre - -	10	3		
	234	5		

HULDIPOOKRE 3d road, by Doarſinny Paſs			
—Gopalnapour in Harrierpour road - -	179	7	
Saſeelah - - -	8	6	
Paunraw - -	8	0	
Juncaw - - -	13	4	
Tooluck - -	18	0	Doarſinny Defile.
Aſnaha - -	5	0	
Guidee Gaut - -	5	0	
Ouleedy - - -	1	4	
Gallegur - -	1	6	
Cuſſumbundy - -	7	2	
Huldipookre - -	9	4	
	258	1	
HURRYAL			
Cullum in Dewangunge 2d road - -	63	0	
Teermuſſundy -	9	6	
Nowgong - -	7	0	
Hurryal - -	3	0	
	82	6	
HYDERABAD, or Soory. See Patna 2d road -	54	5	
JAFFIERGUNGE. See Dacca 1ſt road -	109	0	
JAULDOE. See Junoh Paſs	177	3	
JAGRENAUT. See Ganjam - - -	384	0	

JALALGUNGE				
Burradirga in Rungpour 2d road - - -	134	6		
Jalalgunge - -	8	0		
	142	6		
JANGUIRA. See Patna 1st road - - -	161	2		
JANPOUR. See Harrierpour - - -	175	3		
JARBERY				
Cantoonagur in Dellamcotta road - -	126	0		
Gurnabary - -	11	4	Teestah R.	fer.
Jarbery - - -	5	5		
	143	1		
JAYNAGUR. See Backergunge - - -	119	1		
JELLINGHY				
Azimgunge in Backergunge road - -	19	0	Culcully R.	ford
Jellinghy - - -	10	0		
	29	0		
JELLASORE. See Ganjam	192	0		
JELPIGORY				
Baccally haut, in Bykontpour road - -	177	6		
Jelpigory - -	6	7	Teestah R.	fer.
	184	5		

JENNIDAH. See Culna in Jeſſore - -	87	4		
JESSORE, or Moorley. See Jeſſore Culna -	116	2		
INDOS. See Huldypookre 1ſt road - -	91	4		
JOOGDYA				
Colinda in Iſlamabad road	247	5		
Joogdya - - -	8	4		
	256	1		
JOYPOUR. See Junoh Paſs - - -	162	3		
JUGHIGOPA. See Goalparah - -	246	7		
JUMMUCANDY. See Burdwan - -	22	3		
JUNGLEBARY. See Silhet 1ſt road -	208	6		
JUNGIPOUR				
Churka, in Sooty 2d road	24	6		
Jungipour - -	2	0		
	26	6		

LUCKIDUAR Paſs, in Bootan				
Dewangunge, in Dellamcotta road - -	153	3		
Saibgunge, or *Raymgunge*	11	6	Goggot R.	ford
Luckiduar (page 43) -	60	1		
	225	2		
LUSKERPOUR Purgannah				
Pootya Cutchery. See Dewangunge 2d road -	41	2		
MADDAPOUR, Cutchery of Janguirpour. See Dinagepour 2d road	68	0		
MAHMUDPOUR. See Gopaulgunge - -	122	0		
MAHRAJEGUNGE, or Cuttupgunge in Purneah				
MAULDAH, in Purneah 1ſt road - - -	70	1		
Mahrajegunge (page 44.)	89	1		
	159	2		
MAISSEY. See Bettyah 2d road - -	310	5		
MANGEE. See Suagra	329	0		
MANBOOM. See Singboom - - -	152	7		

MALDUAR Purgannah				
Meerjaſerra, in Mahrajegunge road - -	107	5		
Malduar Cutchery (Rahny) (p. 61.) - -	33	0		
	140	5		
MAULDAH. See Purneah 1ſt road - -	70	1		
MEENKOOT. See Dellamcotta - -	20	6		
MIDNAPOUR. See Ganjam - - -	146	0		
MIRJANAGUR				
Runnagaut, in Calcutta 2d road - - -	79	0		
Sirinagur - -	11	2		
Chandpara - -	9	0		
Chandurya - -	11	3	Iſſamot R.	fer.
Bidaboxa - -	6	6	Nullah	fer.
Mirjanagur - -	9	1	Cobbaduck R.	fer.
	126	4		
MOBOG Gaut, in Birboom				
Purtabpour, in Noony 2d road - - -	60	4		
Baharow - -	5	4		
Mobog Gaut - -	5	4		
	71	4		
MOISHPOUR. See Monghir 3d road - -	40	0		

JUNOH Pafs.				
ROGONATPOUR, in Burwa road - -	125	7		
Collabunny - -	8	4		
Sinkbazar - -	8	4		
Lucdaw - - -	7	6		
Joypour - -	8	4		
Jauldoe - -	15	0		
Sillee - - -	12	0		
Junoh - -	14	4		
	200	5		
ISLAMABAD, or Chittigong 1ft road -				
Hajygunge, in Dacca 2d road - - -	124	5		
Hakeempour - -	9	4		
Rajapour - -	5	2		
Pulyculla - -	8	0	Nullah	fer.
Noorpour - -	6	4	Ganges R. & a N.	fers.
ISLAMABAD (page 37. and 78) - -	161	2		
	315	1		
ISLAMABAD 2d road, by Dacca				
Allynya, in Comilla road	190	4		
Coweddy - -	9	0	Gomut R.	fer.
Chandrahaut - -	7	7	3 Nullahs	2 fers 1 for.
Gunganagur - -	8	5		
Monohargunge - -	12	2	Dackitya N.	fer.
Delluah - -	12	5		
Mahmud Allyhaut -	10	2	Little Fenny	fer.
Meerjapour - -	11	7		
ISLAMABAD, as before	53	6		
	316	6		
KARNOWL. See Bettyah 1ft road - -	335	6		

KEERPOY. See Radnagur	116	5	
KISHENAGUR. See Calcutta 2d road - -	59	6	
KOONDAH			
Petrabad, in Burwah road	184	3	
* *Goleea* - - -	8	4	
* *RAMGUR* - -	12	0	Dummoodah R. ford
Koondah (page 41) -	81	2	
	286	1	
KYRANTY. See Dellamcotta - - -	205	7	
LACARACOONDA. See Burwah - -	78	1	
LUCHMYPOUR, in Jungleterry			
Cudhar, in Monghir 2d road - - -	148	7	
Luchmypour - -	3	4	
	152	3	
LUCKIPOUR, in Dacca Province. See Islamabad 1st road - -	217	7	
LUCKIPOUR, in Bootan			
Guntong, in Luckiduar road - - -	206	4	
Injerra - - -	14	0	
Luckipour - -	6	4	
	22[illegible]	0	

MONGULHAUT. See Buxaduar - -	165	3		
MONGULCOTE. See Burdwan 2d road -	54	0		
MOODUPOUR, in Pookareah - - -				
Nulshi Imaumpour, in Pucculoe road - -	107	1		
Dubya Gaut - -	2	6	Joobnee R.	fer.
Gopalgunge - -	5	0	2 Nallahs	{ 1fer. 1for.
Moodupour - -	6	0		
	120	7		
MOORLEY, or Jessore. See Jessore Culna -	116	2		
MORADBAUG. See Sooty 2d road - -	4	0		
MULFUTGUNGE				
Noorpour, in Islamabad 1st road - - -	153	7		
Nunkissergunge -	13	6	Nullah	ford
Mulfutgunge - -	8	2	Calligonga R.	fer.
	175	7		
MURCHA. See Rungpour 1st road - -	18	2		
MUSTAN-GUR				
Ghiabunder, in Rungpour 3d road - -	79	5		
Mustan-Gur - -	12	7		
	92	4		

MONGHIR, 1ſt road by Terriagully. See Patna 1ſt road - -	182	1		
MONGHIR, 2d road by Birboom, &c. -				
Deogur, in Patna 2d road	134	4		
MONGHIR (page 46)	90	3		
	224	7		
MONGHIR, 3d road by Patchwarry				
Teretcoona - -	5	6	Coſſimbazar R.	ford
Great Rumna -	6	4		
Sonkoe - - -	9	0		
Baderbour - -	14	0		
Egwarbarry - -	3	6		
Moiſhpour - -	1	0		
Utcherya - -	5	0		
‡ *Patchwarry* -	13	2	Banſli R.	ford
Gagur Paſs - -	5	4		
Saitbank, or Burmuſſeah-hill - - -	6	5	Nullah	ford
Dowdand - -	6	6		
‡ Gunjoorya - -	4	4		
Darra - - -	13	6		
Bowſee - - -	6	3		
Bogarya - -	8	4	Chundun N.	ford
Chilkore - - -	7	6		
Noorgunge - -	1	3		
Kinwar - - -	5	0		
Belhary - -	6	4		
Tarrapour - -	6	5	Bunwa N.	ford
Paharpour (direct) -	12	2		
Rampour - -	7	0		
MONGHIR - -	6	0		
	162	6		

‡ Theſe are the only halting places between Moiſhpour and Darra.

NABOBGUNGE. See Dellamcotta - -	32	3		
NAGORE, or Birboom. See Patna 2d road -	70	5		
CHUTA NAGPOUR, or *DOESAH*. See Burwah	171	6		
NARSINGUR. See Huldipookre - - -	199	5		
NARANGUR. See Ganjam	165	3		
NARANGUNGE. See Fringybazar - -	174	2		
NATTORE. See Dewangunge 2d road -	51	3		
NAUTPOUR. See Ammerpour - - -	191	4		
NISHANPOUR. See Dellamcotta - -	73	5		
NOGONG (Cutchery of Barbuckpour). See Rungpour 1st road -	67	0		

NOORNAGUR				
Gowrypour, in Comillah road - - -	196	4		
Salyacondy - -	6	0	Nullah	ford
Tulah - - -	9	4	Gomut R.	fer.
Mokimpour - -	7	0	Nullah	ford
Noornagur - -	9	0	Ditto	ford
	228	0		
NOONY, 1st road by Sarhaut, &c.				
Bugoo, in Darra 2d road	131	0		
Noony - - -	7	5		
	138	5		
NOONY, 2d road by Dobagaut				
Bajitpour, in Patna 2d road	42	3		
Dyoucha - -	7	5		
Purtabpour - -	10	4		
Dobagaut - -	2	5		
Futtapour - -	9	5	Nullah	ford
Doomkah - -	9	0		
Lagwoon - -	7	0		
Amerpour - - -	6	0		
Noony - - -	5	4		
	100	2		
NOONY, 3d road by Patchwarry - -				
Patchwarry, in Monghir 3d road - -	59	2		
Dengah Pass - -	6	2		
Luckersurra Pass -	3	5		
Amrah - - -	6	1		
Sarmee - - -	5	0		
Noony - - -	9	4		
	89	6		
NOANGONG. See Awmore	39	2		

NOTAGUR Paſs. See Huldipookre 1ſt road -	205	1		
NOWADAH. See Patna 3d road - -	230	4		
NOWGONG. See Hurryall	79	6		
NUDDEAH				
Jahanagore, in Calcutta 1ſt road - - -	54	4		
Nuddeah - - -	3	1	Nullah	ford
	57	5		
NULHATTY				
Sonkee, in Monghir 3d road	21	2		
Coytah - - -	5	4		
Nulhatty - -	8	0		
	34	6		
NULDINGA. See Jeſſore Culna - - -	95	6		
NULSHI Imaumpour. See Pucculoe - -	107	1		
NURILAPOUR. See Dacca 2d road - -	131	5		
OKERAH, or Seergur. See Singboom - -	90	1		

OLYAPOUR. See Curyagong - - -	147	6		
OUDANULLA. See Patna 1st road - -	65	6		
PACHETE. See Burwah	117	6		
PALGUNGE				
Serampour, in Curruckdeah 2d road - -	153	7		
Palgunge - - -	8	5		
	162	4		
PALAMOW				
RAMGUR, in Koondah road - -	207	1		
PALAMOW (page 53)	124	0		
	331	1		
PARADANGA, in Bittrebund. See Bisnee -	173	7		
PATNA, 1st road by Terriagully				
Bomineah -	8	8		
PATNA (page 55) -	273	2		
	281	5		
PATNA, 2d road by Birboom				
Callyongunge - -	13	5		
Seerpour (Jillee) - -	6	2	2 Nullahs	fors.
Boudgong - -	8	1		
	28	0		

(Pattergotta continued) -	18	6		
Cassimpour - -	4	1	Nullah	fer.
Muddupour (Talipabads)	4	5		
Callyacure - -	6	5		
Curypara - -	1	3		
Pattergotta - -	8	2		
	43	0		
PIALAPOUR				
Callatyah - -	9	4	Boorygonga R.	fer.
Saapour - - -	9	[illegible]	{ Dollaterry R. and 1 Nullah }	fer.
Sunegar - - -	5	2	Nullah	fer.
Pialapour - -	7	0		
	31	1		
PLASSEY. See Cutwa	168	1		
POINTY				
Terriagully, in Benares 1st road - - -	269	2		
Pointy - - -	8	0		
	277	2		
POOTYA, in Luskerpour				
NATTORE, in Mauldah road - - -	130	1		
Chandpour - -	5	0		
Pootya - - -	5	1		
	140	2		
POOKARYAH. See Bisnee	86	5		
PUBNA. See Benares 1st road - - -	98	7		

POOTYA (Cutcherry of Luſkerpour.) See Dewangunge 2d road -	41	2		
POOKARYA (Mudoopour Cutcherry of ditto.) See Mudoopour - -	120	7		
PUBNA Nazirpour. See Dacca 1ſt road -	66	0		
PUCCULOE, in Attyah Cullum, in Dewangunge 2d road - -	63	0		
Beeaſs - - -	8	1		
Tarwas - - -	7	4		
Comully - -	12	0	Foolju R.	fer.
Cauleah - - -	9	4	Coni R.	fer.
Nulſhi Imaumpour -	6	0		
Potul - - -	7	0	Joobnee R.	fer.
Suntoſh - - -	10	6	2 Nullahs	ford
Attyah - - -	4	2	Lojung R.	fer.
PUCCULOE - -	8	2	2 Nullahs	ford
	136	3		
PUCCULOE, 2d road by Belcuchy				
Tarwas, as before -	78	5		
Angaroe - - -	8	3		
Burrumcopilea -	5	3	Nullah	fer.
Dowlatpour - -	5	6	Ditto	fer.
Belcuchy - -	7	1	Ditto	ford
Gundruckpour -	9	3	Coni and Joobnee Rs.	fer.
Suntoſh - - -	4	7		
Attyah - -	4	2	Lojung R.	fer.
PUCCULOE - -	8	2	2 Nullahs	ford
	132	0		

PURRUAH. See Mahraje-gunge - - -	77	3		
PURNEAH, 1st road by Mauldah				
Chappigunge, in Dellam-cotta road - -	37	7		
PURNEAH (page 60)	106	7		
	144	6		
PURNEAH, 2d road by Ter-riagully				
Terriagully, in Patna 1st road - - -	104	3		
Pointy - -	8	0		
Caragolah - -	7	0	Ganges R.	fer.
Gondwarra - -	14	0		
Milkee - - -	11	2		
PURNEAH - -	7	3		
	152	0		
PUTYMAHRY				
Chunapour - -	5	2		
Lowdah - - -	6	3		
Callytulla - -	7	3	Nullah	ford
Batebarya - -	3	2		
Ballitunghy - -	6	0		
Jeatpour - -	9	4	Jellinghy R.	ford
Putymahry - -	6	6		
	44	4		
PUTTYRAM. See Dinage-pour 2d road -	99	6		
RADNAGUR				
Madapour, in Ganjam road	109	7		
Keerpoy - -	6	6		
Radnagur - -	2	0		
	118	5		

RAJANAGUR				
Pattergotta - -	6	0	Boorygonga & Dollaterry R.	fer.
Surajady - -	5	0		
Duckinchargong -	4	3		
Dunconya - -	5	7	Nullah	ford
Nunkissergunge -	3	5		
Rajanagur - -	5	4	Calligonga R.	fer.
	30	3		
RAJEMAL 1st road. See Benares 1st road -	237	1		
RAJEMAL 2d road. See Patna 3d road -	239	4		
RAJEGUNGE, or Dinagepour. See Purneah 2d road - - -	202	7		
RAMGUR. See Palamow	375	3		
RANGAMATTY. See Bisnee - -	232	3		
RAYMGUNGE, or Saibgunge. See Dellamcotta - -	244	7		
ROGONAUTPOUR. See Doesah - -	297	2		

ROHANPOUR, or Rahnpour				
Gomastapour, in Purneah 1st road - -	46	4		
Rohanpour - -	4	4		
	51	0		
ROGONATPOUR. See Burwa - -	125	7		
ROONAY. See Chacki 2d road - - -	134	7		
ROTAH Pass				
Decgur, in Patna 2d road	134	4		
Chandun - -	9	3	Nullah	ford
Cutteryah - -	10	0	Ditto	ford
Cosmow - - -	10	0		
Rotah Pass - -	9	2		
	173	1		
ROTAS GUR				
Tickarry, in Benares 2d road	286	1		
ROTAS GUR (page 62)	71	6	Soane R.	ford
	357	7		
ROYPOUR				
Burra Seringa, in Huldipookre 1st road -	149	5		
Roypour - - -	5	2	Cassai R.	ford
	154	7		
RUMNAH. See Monghir 3d road - - -	12[illegible]	2		

RUNGPOUR, 1st road by Buddaul				
Cuttorah - -	2	0		
RUNGPOUR (page 63)	140	0		
	142	0		
RUNGPOUR, 2d road by Goragot				
Bowanygunge, as before	48	7		
RUNGPOUR (page 64)	100	2		
	149	1		
RUNGPOUR, 3d road by Seebgunge				
Carree, as before -	72	4		
Ghiabunder - -	7	1	Nagore N.	ford
Punderaticky - -	11	4	Ditto	ford
Seebgunge - -	4	2	Nullah	ford
Gobingunge - -	11	0	Currattya R.	ford
Palaſbery - -	11	0		
Haatybunder - -	7	4		
RUNGPOUR, as before	23	7		
	148	6		
RUTTUNGUNGE. See Dacca 1ſt road -	99	0		
RYNABAD				
Culna (Jeſſore) -	148	4		
Jerryah - - -	10	6		
Rynabad - -	4	2		
	163	4		
SANASHYGOTTA				
DINAGEPOUR, in Dellamcotta road -	114	4		
Sanaſhygotta (page 65)	76	1		
	190	5		

SAIBGUNGE, or Raymgunge. See Dellamcotta	165	1		
SANTIPOUR				
Amboa, in Calcutta road	69	5		
Santipour - -	5	7	Hoogly R.	fer.
	75	4		
SARHAUT. See Patna 2d road - - -	111	0		
SASERAM. See Benares 2d road - -	345	5		
SEEDLEY				
Barriapour, in Bettyah 2d road - - -	221	2		
Seedley (page 66) -	129	4		
	350	6		
SEERGUR, or Okerah. See Singboom - -	90	1		
SEWAAN, or Allygunge				
Moneab, in Benares 1st road	302	7		
Cheeran - -	6	7	Ganges R.	fer.
CHUPRAH - -	7	6		
Jaitpour - - -	13	3		
Bagorah - - -	11	3		
Hussar - -	5	6		
Sewaan - - -	7	2		
	355	2		
SEEBGUNGE. See Rungpour 3d road - -	95	3		

SEERPOUR, in Mahmanshy. See Dewangunge 2d road	88	2		
SEERPOUR (Jille.) See Patna 2d road -	19	7		
SERAMPOUR, in Bahar. See Curruckdea 2d road	153	7		
SERAMPOUR (Danish factory) - -				
Ghyretty, in Calcutta 1st road - - -	101	6		
- *Serampour* - -	4	0		
	105	6		
SHAZADPOUR				
Nowgong, in Hurryal road	79	6		
Ghyhutta - - -	7	3		
Hulletgur - -	6	2	Foolju R.	fer.
Shazadpour - -	6	0		
	99	3		
SHEERGOTTY				
Gayah, in Benares 2d road	270	7		
Battee - - -	6	6		
Goruah - -	11	6		
Sheergotty - -	10	0		
	299	3		
SHILBERIS. See Buggorah	93	5		
SIBNIBAS				
KISHENAGUR, in Calcutta 2d road - -	59	6		

(Sibnibas continued)	59	6		
Ilaburrya - - -	5	2		
Sibnibas - - -	8	0		
	73	0		
SICLYGULLY. See Patna 1st road -	91	5		
SILLEE. See Junoh Pass	189	3		
SILHET, 1st road by Seerpour				
Golabarry, in Dewangunge 2d road - -	117	4		
Ilajypour - -	9	0	Jenni R.	ford
Buziapour - -	6	2		
Pykerhaut - -	10	6		
Eetal - - -	5	3		
Bygonbary - -	11	2		
Cassergunge - -	9	3	Burrumpooter R.	fer.
Bokinagur - -	10	2	2 Nullahs	ford
Chumaroola - -	10	6	1 Ditto	ford
Murchagunge - -	9	2	1 Ditto	ford
Junglebary - -	9	0		
Panchcownya - -	11	0	Nullah	fer.
Eetna - - -	7	1	Dunnu & Bolee Rs.	fer.
Azmerigunge - -	10	0	{ Lamakerra, & Megna Rivers }	fer.
Banniachung - -	8	1		
Connipour - -	9	4		
Agnah - - -	5	2	Nullah	ford
* Cattyah - - -	11	0		
* Bunbaug - -	10	0	Bussya N.	ford
* *SILHET* - -	9	2	Soormah R.	fer.
	290	0		
SILHET, 2d road by Dacca				
DACCA - - -	164	7		
SILHET (page 69) -	145	6		
	310	5		

SINGBOOM				
Lacaracoonda, in Burwa road - - -	78	1		
Okera, or Seergur -	12	0	Adji R.	ford
Mudjeah - -	11	0	Dummoodah R.	ford
Cooſtilla - - -	8	4		
Chatna - - -	12	0		
Condeacoora - -	5	0		
Ranjeetpour - -	8	0	Dalkiſor	ford
Baumundya - -	5	5		
Pyratelly - -	9	2		
Manboom - -	3	3	Caſſai R.	ford
Mudjehara - -	10	0		
Muccroo - -	8	0		
Lukenpour - -	8	0		
Malkee - - -	9	0		
Muroo - -	8	1		
Muſſerah - -	9	6	Subunreka R.	ford
Patcoom - -	5	0		
* *Singboom* - -	26	0	by Banſa Paſs	
	233	6		
SOOPOUR				
Aſſoah, in Burdwan 2d road	28	4		
Curoondah - -	8	2		
Omdarrah - -	11	4		
Surrool - - -	6	5		
Soopour - - -	3	1		
	58	0		
SOORY, or Hyderabad. See Patna 2d road -	54	5		
SOOTY, 1ſt road. See Patna 1ſt road - -	35	1		
SOOTY, 2d road				
Moradbaug - -	4	0	Coſſimbuzar R.	ford
Sooty (page 73) -	32	2		
	36	2		

SUAGRA				
CHUPRAH, in Sewaan road	317	4		
Suagra (page 73) -	57	5		
	375	1		
SULTANPOUR Aurung				
Purrua, in Mahrajegunge road - - -	77	3		
Sultanpour - -	11	5		
	89	0		
SULTANABAD (Birkooty Cutcherry)				
See Birkooty - -	39	0		
SUJATPOUR. See Silhet 2d road - -	253	4		
SUNAMOOKY Aurung				
Mongulkote, in Burdwan 2d road - - -	54	0		
Dignagur - -	15	6		
Futtapour - -	15	0		
Sunamooky - -	7	6	Dummoodah R. ford	
	92	4		
SUMMUTGUR. See Calcutta 1st road -	58	6		
SURYA. See Patna 2d road	122	6		
SURROOL. See Soopour	54	7		

SURROOPOUR Purganah				
DINAGEPOUR, in Dellamcotta road -	114	4		
Bagduar Gaut - -	8	6	- -	2 fers
Comergunge - -	10	3		
Samgunge Cutchery -	10	0		
	143	5		
SURDAH. See Chatmol	37	4		
SUTALURY				
Madapaſſah, in Backergunge road - -	199	0		
Mogoſſy - -	7	4	2 Nullahs	ford
Sutalury - - -	5	0	1 ditto	ford
	211	4		
TAMLOOK				
Culna, in Calcutta 1ſt road	66	7		
Böenchee - -	12	0		
Kiſſabatty - -	6	0		
Deneacolly - -	8	0		
Bilegur - - -	8	2		
Kiſtnagur - -	10	4		
Omptah - - -	13	0		
Baugnan - -	9	0	Dummoodah R.	fer.
Bynapour - -	5	0		
Tamlook - - -	9	0	Roopnaram R. & 1 N.	fer.
	147	5		
TARRAPOUR, 1ſt road by Terriagully. See Curruckpour 1ſt road -	168	0		
2d road by Birboom. See Monghir 2d road - -	184	7		

TAUJEPOUR, in Purneah. See Mahrajegunge	135	3		
TENGÜA (Cutchery of Islamabad Purgannah				
Seebgunge, in Rungpour 3d road - - -	95	3		
Curryabadder - -	13	0	Nullua N.	ford
Tengüa - - -	8	0	Bangalla R.	fer.
	116	3		
TERRIAGULLY. See Patna 1st road -	104	3		
TICKARRY. See Benares 2d road - -	286	1		
TIPERAH, or Comillah. See Comillah -	224	1		
TOMAR, or Tamar				
Jauldoe, in Junoh road	177	3		
* *Tomar* - - -	15	0		
	192	3		
TOONRY. See Curruckdea 2d road - -	139	7		
TORROFF				
Sunerampour, in Silhet 2d road - - -	221	0		
Torroff (page 6) -	42	4		
	263	4		

TOREE			
Tikoo, in Palamow road	274	5	
Tikoo Paſs - -	3	6	
Toree - - -	9	2	
	287	5	
TUREE, or Tuer in Jungle-terry			
Sarbaut, in Patna 2d road	111	0	
Luckorya - -	8	4	
Mudwun - -	3	6	
Banka - - -	4	5	
Turee - - -	4	6	
	132	5	
TURKI. See Bettyah 2d road - - -	295	7	

TABLES OF ROADS,

FROM

P A T N A,

TO ALL THE PRINCIPAL PLACES IN

BENGAL AND BAHAR.

Expreſſing the Length of the Stages, and the Number and Situation of the Fords and Ferries.

TABLES OF ROADS,

From PATNA, to all the principal Places in BENGAL and BAHAR.

Names of Places.	distances in Miles and Furl.		Rivers and Nullahs to be crossed.	ford or ferry.
ALLIGUNGE, or Sewaan.				
See Hoseepour -	73	4		
AMMERPOUR, in Morung				
HAJYPOUR - -	4	6	Ganges R.	fer.
Burni Choky - -	9	3		
Mow - - -	6	3	Byar N.	ford
Sukee - - -	9	6		
Pusah - - -	12	3	Little Gunduck R.	ford
Chuckmussey - -	5	0		
Tarry - - -	2	5	Buckya R.	ford
DURBUNGAH -	10	0	Bogmutty R.	ford
Berhi - - -	5	3	Comlah R.	ford
Bowara - - -	11	0		
Merjapour - -	8	2		
Kemgur - -	10	5		
Lokobar - - -	14	0		
* *AMMERPOUR* -	28	0		
	137	4		
AMAROUD. See Burwa	95	1		
ARVAL. See page 9.	45	0		
ARRAH. See page 8.	38	0		

ATTYA. See Dacca 3d road	391	1	
AYTURAH. See Calcutta 3d road	200	4	
AZMERIGUNGE. See Silhet - -	470	3	
BACKERGUNGE			
MOORSHEDABAD, in Calcutta 1st road - -	281	5	
Backergunge (page 84)	215	2	
	496	7	
BAGGOR, or Delour Gaut 1st road. See Calcutta 3d road - -	75	5	
BAGGOR 2d road, Cuttree in Calcutta 2d road -	56	6	
Varasellygunge - -	5	0	
Row - - -	9	3	
Baggor, or Delour Gaut	6	2	
	77	3	
BAHAR. See Calcutta 2d road - - -	44	0	
BALGUDA, 1st road. See Chacki - -	70	6	
BALGUDA, 2d road by Bahar			
BAHAR, in Calcutta 2d road - - -	44	0	

(Balguda continued)	44	0		
Palany - - -	8	6		
Cooserah - - -	6	6	Sacry N.	ford
Sheikpour - - -	7	4		
Massorah - -	6	4		
Balguda - - -	9	2		
	82	6		
BALASORE. See Ganjam	390	0		
By Calcutta	541	2		
BAR. See Calcutta 1st road - - -	37	5		
BAULEAH. See Hurryal	293	3		
BEERA. See Kisselpour, or Cosselpour - -	269	3		
BELLIAH				
Bar, in Calcutta 1st road	37	5		
Rajouly - - -	5	5	Ganges R.	fer.
Dalalpour - -	6	6	Nullah	fer.
Tigrah - - -	5	4	Ditto	fer.
Howaspour - -	6	4		
Serra - - -	6	0		
Belliah - - -	12	1		
	80	1		
BELCUCHY - -				
Pongash, in Dacca 3d road	357	7		
Cauleah - - -	6	6		
Belcuchy - - -	8	4		
	373	1		

BENARES, 1st road by Buxar. (See page 8)				
BENARES, 2d road by Sasseram. (See page 8)	165	4		
BERNAGUR, in Purneah				
Seral, in Purneah 2d road	123	4		
Mynatnagur - -	8	4	Gogary R.	fer.
Niahnagur - -	11	2		
Jenjeree - - -	4	0		
Purwanpour - -	8	0		
Mulygunge - -	7	4		
Bernagur - -	11	0	Nullah	ford
	173	6		
BERNAGUR, 2d road. See Purneah 3d road -	162	2		
BETTYAH (page 10)	100	0		
BEYHAR, or Coos Beyhar, 1st road. See Buxaduar	386	2		
BEYHAR 2d road, by Purneah				
Colgong, in Calcutta 1st road - - -	156	6		
Baidur Chokey -	3	4		
Koorgunge - -	10	0		
Pointee - -	3	0		
Caragola - -	7	0	Ganges R.	fer.
Gondwarra - -	14	0		
Milkee - -	11	2	Old Coosy R.	ford
	205	4		

(Beyhar 2d road, continued)	205	4		
PURNEAH - -	7	3		
Dubelly Gaut - -	9	4	Dubelly R.	ford
Purſony - -	6	4	Nullah	ford
Pokareeah - -	6	6	Ditto	ford
Himmutnagur - -	8	2	2 Nullahs	ford
Mahrarajegunge -	7	4	{ Conkiand / Mahanada }	fors.
Kiſhengunge - -	4	2		
Chainpour - -	7	4		
Peergunge - -	5	3		
Burbarry - -	5	6	Nagore N.	ford
Akalagur - -	6	6		
Tarrabary - -	7	3	Tangan N.	ford
Burragong - -	3	6		
Dum - - -	6	6		
Teeſta River - -	9	0	- - -	fer.
Dewangunge - -	4	0		
Cheerabeeja - -	8	4		
Calpauny - -	8	0		
Haatybunder - -	8	0		
Lolbazar - -	9	0		
Callygunge - -	7	2	2 Nullahs	fors.
Bogurbarry - -	6	6	Old Durla R.	ford
Beyhar Cantonments -	6	7	{ Durla R.	ford
BEYHAR - - -	2	5	Manſhi R.	fer.
			Toreſha R. }	fer.
	368	7		
BIRBOOM, or Nagore. See Calcutta 2d road	209	7		
BIRKOOTY, in Sultanabad				
MONGHIR, in Calcutta, 1ſt road - -	99	4		
Rampour - -	6	0		
Paharpour - -	7	0		
Tarrapour - -	12	2	Bunwa N.	ford
Belharee - -	6	5		
	141	3		

(Birkooty continued)	141	3		
Kinwar - -	6	4		
Noorgunge - -	5	0		
Chilkore - -	1	3		
Bogaryah - -	7	6	Chundun N.	ford
Bowſee - - -	8	4		
Darra - - -	6	3	Chere N.	ford
‡ Gunjoorya - -	13	6		
Dowdand - -	4	4		
Saintbank, or Burmuſſea Hill - - -	6	6		
Gagur Paſs - -	6	5	Nullah	ford
‡ *Patchwarry* - -	5	4		
Utcherya - -	13	2	Banſli R.	ford
Moiſhpour - -	5	0		
Egwarbarry - -	1	0		
Birkooty - - -	3	0		
	226	2		

‡ Theſe are the only halting places between Darra and Moiſhpour.

BISNEE				
RAJEMAL, in Calcutta 1ſt road - -	209	3		
Aamgatch - -	10	6	Ganges R.	fer.
Cotwally - -	6	7		
MAULDAH - -	2	7	Mahanada R.	fer.
Sawan - - -	9	7	Tangan R. and 1 Nullah	fers.
Ponkakpukre - -	11	0		
Hopponya Gaut -	6	0	Purnabubah R.	fer.
Niſhanpour - -	4	0		
Sapaar - - -	4	2		
Sunderpour - -	4	4		
Balloo Gaut - -	10	2	Attri R.	fer.
Durool - - -	10	0		
Buxygunge - -	6	5		
Nabobgunge - -	13	0	Nullah	ford
Cooſugary - -	6	6	2 Ditto	ford
Mullung - -	11	4		
	327	5		

(Bisnee continued)	327	5		
RUNGPOUR - -	7	0	Goggot R.	fer.
Cowanya - -	9	0	Monaash N.	ford
Ponga - - -	9	2	Teesta N.	ford
Nawassy - -	9	3	Durla & Neelcomer	fer.
Paradanga - -	3	6	Nullah	ford
Poonkur - - -	10	2	Sunecoss R.	fer.
Bisnee (page 12.) -	97	2		
	473	4		
BISRAMPOUR. See Palamow 1st road -	158	1		
BISSUNPOUR. See Ganjam - - -	254	5		
BITTREBUND Purganah, *Paradanga* Cutchery. See Bisnee - - -	303	2		
BOGLIPOUR. See Calcutta 1st road -	137	2		
BOGWANGOLA				
Dewanserai, in Calcutta 1st road - - -	265	2		
Sankral - - -	4	0		
Bogwangola - -	7	2		
	276	4		
BOGGAH				
BETTYAH (page 10)	100	0		
Mutteah - -	13	5		
Chandapour - -	15	2		
Boggah - - -	6	4		
	135	3		

BOGARYAH. See Birkooty - -	156	6		
BOOSNAH. See Backergunge - - -	403	5		
BOUJEPOUR				
Ranaſagur, in Benares 1ſt road - - -	58	4		
Boujepour - -	12	4		
	71	0		
BOWANIPOUR in Purneah. See Purneah 2d road - - -	156	0		
BURDWAN. See Calcutta 2d road - -	279	3		
BURHAMPOUR Cantonments				
MOORSHEDABAD, in Calcutta 1ſt road - -	281	5		
Burhampour - -	5	3	Coſſimbuzar R.	2fer.
	287	0		
BURRABOOM				
Chaculturry, in Midnapour 2d road - -	237	6		
Burraboom - -	14	0		
	251	6		
BURWA				
Futwa - - -	8	6		

(Burwa continued)	8	6		
Hilsah - - -	14	6		
Mahrajegunge -	8	6		
Islampour - -	5	2		
Olassgunge - -	5	4		
Nawdiah - -	6	7		
Mugsoodpour - -	9	1		
Gayah - - -	10	2	Fulgoo R.	ford
Hattyah - - -	11	2		
Assuerry - -	6	0		
Amaroud - -	8	5		
Kadely - -	7	0		
Luseennugh - -	6	4		
Chitrah, or *Chetrah* -	11	4		
Latewah - -	10	4		
Jubbra - - -	7	2		
Barcattu - -	9	4		
Kohmur - -	6	2		
Odeygunge - -	8	4		
Tikoo Pass - -	10	0		
Tikoo-Monatco - -	3	6		
Ilcera - - -	6	2		
Loburdega - -	6	2	Nullah	ford
Seenah - - - -	3	4		
Bootee - - -	7	4		
Cotamutty - -	5	6		
Nohnee - -	4	2		
* *Jargi* Pass - -	6	0		
* Solamee - -	5	4		
BURWA - -	7	4		
	227	7		
BUXAR. See page 8. -	85	1		
BUXADUAR, 1st road by Rungpour				
RUNGPOUR, in Bisnee road - - -	334	5		
Buxaduar (page 16) -	95	0		
	429	5		

CALCUTTA, 1ſt road by Moorſhedabad -				
Futwa - - -	8	6		
Bykontpour - -	4	5		
Mogulpurra - -	6	3		
Semmya - -	8	3		
Bar - - -	9	4		
Punerack - - - -	5	5		
Shunar - - -	7	4		
Derriapour - -	5	5		
Doomarra - -	6	1		
Jaintpour - -	4	0		
Rampour - -	7	5	3 Nullahs	1 for. 2 fer.
Surajegurra - -	7	5		
Singhya Nulla -	10	6		
MONGHIR - -	7	0		
Seetacoon - -	5	0		
Goorgut Nulla -	11	6	- -	fer.
Janguira - - -	4	1		
Sultangunge - -	2	3		
Champernagur - -	12	1	Nullah	ford
BOGLIPOUR - -	2	3		
Goga Nulla - -	11	0		
Teermahony Nulla -	5	2	- -	fer.
Colgong - - -	3	2	Nullah	ford
Pialapour - -	11	4		
Shahabad - -	6	0		
Terriogully - -	3	0		
Gongaperſaud - -	4	4		
Siclygully - -	8	2		
Muſſaw - - - -	9	3		
RAJEMAL - - -	10	0		
Oudanulla - - -	6	4		
Furruckabad - -	11	6		
Downapour - -	7	6	Nullah	ford
Sooty - -	11	1	2 ditto	fors.
Comrah - -	8	2	Coſſimbuzar R.	ford
Dewanſerai - -	10	4	Nullah	ford
Bomineah -	8	0		
MOORSHEDABAD (*Mootyjyl*) - -	8	3		
	281	5		

Calcutta, 1ſt road, continued)	281	5		
CALCUTTA, Old Fort, (page 92) -	118	5		
	400	2		

CALCUTTA, 2d road by Chacki Paſs				
Futwa - - -	8	6		
Hilſah - -	14	6	Mahany R.	ford
Suan - - -	10	0	2 Nullahs	fors.
BAHAR - -	10	4	Banourah N.	ford
Cuttree - - -	12	6	Panchanny N.	ford
Chuckwa - -	3	2	Sacry N.	ford
Dummoul - -	12	3		
Iſlamnagur - -	5	5		
Lechwar - - -	6	4		
Guidere - - -	13	0		
Jundoo - - -	7	4		
Sonah - - -	4	4		
Dumree - - -	2	4		
Betteeah Gaut -	6	2		
Chacki, or Fort Haſtings	7	2		
Aſnah - - -	3	6		
Silpherry - -	4	4		
Sirſah - - -	8	0		
Deogur, or Deugur -	4	2		
Surya - - -	11	6		
Sarbaut - - -	11	6		
Operbanda - -	8	0		
Aſnah - - -	10	0		
Doley - - -	11	3		
Doodapauny - -	5	3		
NAGORE, or Birboom	5	5		
Burſaul Gaut - -	4	1		
Niagaut - - -	2	4		
Dubrajepour - -	6	7		
Kiſtnagur - -	3	1		
Goorſhya - -	10	3	Cupi N.	ford
Illambazar - -	3	6		
Curnagore - -	7	0	Adji R.	ford
	247	5		

(Calcutta, 2d road continued - -	247	5		
Oufgong - -	5	4		
Dignagur - -	6	2		
Bunpafs - - -	7	2		
BURDWAN Factory -	12	6	Curree N.	ford
Pyowrah - - -	3	4		
Purlah - - -	5	6		
Selimabad - -	7	7		
Deneacolly - -	10	2	2 Nullahs	fors.
Bundipour - -	10	0		
Chunditulla - -	12	1	2 Nullahs	{ 1 for. 1 fer.
CALCUTTA - -	12	0	Hoogly R.	fer.
	340	7		

CALCUTTA, 3d road by Curruckdeah				
BAHAR, as before -	44	0		
Gereek - - -	11	1		
Nowadah - -	10	5	Coory N.	ford
Burdhoo, or Berertha -	3	0	Ditto	ford
Baggor, or Delour Gaut	6	7		
Govinpour - -	4	4	Sacry N.	ford
Seebpour - -	6	4		
Gomah - - -	13	6	Ditto thrice	fords
Soank - - -	4	6	Ditto twice	fords
Kifgoe - - -	8	6	Ditto thrice	fords
Curruckdeah - -	10	3		
Nowadah - -	6	2		
Buraw - - -	11	4		
Serampour - -	6	4		
Panreedy - -	10	6	Burracur R.	ford
Gadee-Toonry - -	3	6		
Hurkutta - -	10	5		
Debbe Yanna - -	9	5		
Paunraw - - -	3	0		
Burmoree - -	6	6	Ditto	ford
Aytura - - -	7	4		
Rajapour - - -	12	4		
	203	0		

(Calcutta, 3d road, continued) - -	203	0		
Okera, or *Seergur* -	10	4		
Puralya - - -	6	0		
Gopaulpour - -	9	4		
Cooksee - - -	5	6		
Mauncore - -	6	4		
Dincgur - -	7	3		
CALCUTTA, as before	81	4		
	340	1		
CARAGOLA. See Beyhar 2d road - -	180	2		
CAUGMAHRY				
Potul, in Dacca 3d road	376	1		
Caugmahry - -	9	4		
	385	5		
CHACKI, or Fort *Hastings* 1st road. See Calcutta 2d road - - -	125	4		
CHACKI, 2d road				
Jaintpour, in Calcutta 1st road - - -	66	4		
Balguda - - -	4	2	2 Nullahs	ford
Rampour - -	5	2		
Ramsoor Pass - -	4	0		
Boscoon Nulla - -	5	0	- -	ford
Mellypour - -	7	0		
Neema - - -	5	0		
Guidore - - -	5	3		
Jundoo - -	7	4		
Sonah - - -	4	4		
Dumree - - -	2	4		
Betteah Gaut - -	6	2		
Chacki - -	7	2		
	130	3		

CHAMPERNAGUR. See Calcutta 1ſt road -	134	7		
CHANDERNAGORE. See Calcutta 1ſt road -	379	0		
CHAMPAH Paſs				
Gaya, in Burwa road -	69	2		
Pawah - - -	10	4		
Laguepour - -	6	4		
Dumra - - -	10	0		
Champah Paſs - -	8	0		
	104	2		
CHATNA. See Ganjam	224	7		
CHAUNKY				
BETTYA (page 10) -	100	0		
Ticoleah - -	10	6		
Saitee - - -	3	4	Suckaroona R.	ford
Rowaree - - -	7	0		
Chaunky - -	7	0		
	128	2		
CHICHACOTTA. See Buxaduar - -	404	6		
CHILKORE. See Birkooty	149	0		
CHILMARY				
Buxigunge, in Biſnee road	296	3		
* Culſy - - -	6	4		
* Rannygunge - -	10	5		
GORAGOT - -	5	0	Curattya R.	
	318	4		

(Chilmary continued) -	318	4		
Pannyerbarry - -	8	6	Nulluah N.	ford
Noongola - -	7	o	Goggot R.	fer.
Boggurya - -	7	o	Coolny R.	fer.
Nallagunge - -	8	o	Serri R.	fer.
Chilmary - -	7	1	Teesta N.	ford
	356	3		
CHINSURA				
HOOGLY, in Calcutta 1st road - - -	374	5		
Chinsura - - -	1	6		
	376	3		
CHITTIGONG. The same as Islamabad - -	596	6		
CHITTRA, or Chetra. See Burwa - -	119	5		
CHOWSAR				
Buxar (page 8) -	85	1		
Chowsar - -	6	6		
	91	7		
CHUNARGUR				
Mogulserai, in Benares 2d road -	156	6		
CHUNARGUR -	18	o		
	174	6		
CHUPRAH. See Hoseepour	35	7		
COILURE Gaut. See page 8. - -	29	2		

COLGONG. See Calcutta 1st road - -	156	0		
COMILLAH				
DACCA - -	446	4		
Futtulah - -	6	5	2 Nullahs	fer.
Naraingunge - -	2	6		
Gudjaleah - -	7	2	- -	2 fers
COMILLAH (page 41)	42	[illegible]		
	505	6		
COMERCALLY. See Dacca 2d road - -	353	3		
COOSERAH. See Balguda 2d road - -	59	4		
COOS BEYHAR. See Beyhar - - -	368	[illegible]		
COSSIMBUZAR. See Calcutta 1st road -	284	0		
COTUMBAH				
Daoudnagur (page 8)	67	1		
Piprah Gur - -	11	0		
Serris - - -	10	0		
Curhara - -	7	0		
Cotumbah - -	11	4		
	106	5		
COWAH GAUT				
Dummoul, in Calcutta 2d road - - -	72	2		

(Cowah Gaut continued)	72	2		
Pollay - - -	6	2		
Cowah Gaut - -	5	4		
	84	0		
CURRUCKPOUR				
Mellypour, in Chacki 2d road - - -	92	0		
Pandoo - - -	5	3		
Gourdee - -	4	4		
Milkee - - -	9	6		
CURRUCKPOUR -	5	0		
	116	5		
CURRUCKDEAH. See Calcutta 3d road -	124	2		
CURCHI				
Mow, in Ammerpour road	20	4		
Sehan - - -	6	4		
Barwarry - -	6	2		
Surubdypour - -	10	4	Little Gunduck R.	ford
Surujeputty - -	7	0	Buckiah R.	ford
Dunnore - -	2	6		
Jejuarra - - -	8	4		
Coillee - - -	8	6		
Peperelly - -	10	5		
Parriah - - -	8	3		
Curchi - - -	5	0		
	94	6		
CUTTACK. See Ganjam	496	4		
CUTWA. See Kishenagur	272	2		

DACCA, 1ſt road by Moorſhedabad				
MOORSHEDABAD, in Calcutta 1ſt road - -	281	5		
Hurryſongkor (page 84)	39	6		
DACCA (page 99) -	125	1		
	446	4		
DACCA 2d road, by Hajygunge				
MOORSHEDABAD -	281	5		
Moddapour Pangſa (p. 84)	84	6		
DACCA (page 99) -	80	1		
	446	4		
DACCA 3d road, by Mauldah				
Niſhanpour, in Biſnee road	260	6		
Tilna - - -	6	2		
Seebpour - - -	4	1		
Conchon - - -	4	6	Attri R.	fer.
Saumgunge - -	12	0	Nullah	ford
Jamaulgunge - -	7	6	Ditto	ford
Eetacola - - -	6	6		
Cottal - - -	8	4		
Buggcorah - -	14	0	Nagore R.	ford
Garridah - -	11	0		
Seerpcur - - -	3	0		
Chatterpour Gaut -	6	4	Curratyah R.	fer.
Bagah haut - -	7	6		
Pongaſh - - -	4	6		
Rummatgunge - -	4	4	Iſſamutty R.	fer.
Nulſhi Imaumpour -	6	6	2 Nullahs, 1 fo.	fer.
Potul - - -	7	0	Joobnee R.	fer.
Suntoſh - - -	10	6	2 Nullahs	ford
Attyah - - -	4	2	Lojung R.	fer.
PUCCULOE - -	8	2	2 Nullahs	ford
Mirzahaut - -	6	4		
Candapotul - -	11	4		
Dumroy - - -	6	1		
	423	4		

Place				
(Dacca 3d road continued)	423	4		
Sabaar - - -	6	1	Bunſe R.	fer.
Sampour - - -	4	6	Nullah	fer.
Sibdy haut - -	6	4	4 Rs. & Nullahs	fer.
DACCA - - -	8	0	Nullah	ford
	448	7		
DAOUDNAGUR. See page 8 - -	67	1		
DARRA, in Jungleterry. See Birkooty - -	166	7		
DELOUR, or Baggor Gaut. See Baggor - -	75	5		
DELLAMCOTTA				
Mahrajegunge, in Beyhar 2d road - -	251	3		
Mootyhara - -	7	6	Dunk R.	ford
Derghyeygunge - -	4	0		
Jaſſiergunge - -	7	2		
Haldibarry - -	6	0		
Sonapour - -	8	0		
Titalya - - -	7	0		
Burabary - -	8	0	Dunk R.	ford
Dubonce - -	6	7	Corto R.	ford
Jelpigory - -	12	6		
Durgahaut, or Doonga	3	0	Teeſta R.	fer.
Bottabury - -	4	3		
Fooljerra - -	9	0	Durla R.	ford
Kyranty - - -	6	7		
Entrance of the Hills -	7	4	Ditto	ford
* *Dellamcotta* - -	15	0		
	364	6		
DEOGUR, or Deugur. See Calcutta 2d road	146	0		

	M.	F.		
DEOPOUR				
Serampour, in Calcutta 3d road - - -	148	4		
Deopour - - -	11	2	Usree N.	ford
	159	6		
DEWANGUNGE (in Patladah)				
GORAGOT, in Chilmary road - - -	318	4		
Pannyerbary - -	8	6	Nullah	ford
Iwetepour haut - -	10	4	Goggot R.	fer.
Rottinpour - -	4	5	Monaash N.	ford
Dewangunge - -	10	4	2 Nullahs	fers.
	352	7		
DINAGEPOUR, or Rajegunge				
MAULDAH, in Bisnee road	229	7		
Purrua - - -	7	2		
Addyna Mosque - -	1	4		
Seetul Chokey - -	8	0		
Soeci - - -	6	6		
Pattergotta Tank -	6	0		
Saregunge - -	12	0	Tangan R.	ford
Futtypour - -	6	2		
DINAGEPOUR, or Rajegunge - - -	8	6	Purnabubah R.	fer.
	286	3		
DOBAGAUT, or Muncalgur Pass				
Darra, in Birkooty road	166	7		
Dunwa - - -	11	2		
Kindooah - -	4	0		
Noony - - -	6	6		
Amerpour - -	5	4		
Lagwoon - -	6	0		
Doomkah - -	7	0		
	207	3		

(Dobagaut continued) -	207	3		
Futtypour - - -	9	0		
Dobagaut - -	9	5		
	226	0		
DOESAH, or Chuta Nagpour				
Loburdega, in Burwah road	187	7		
Mudmaunu - -	9	0	Coyle R.	ford
Urkoh - - -	3	4		
Lutdaug - -	4	0		
Seſſei - - -	8	0		
DOESAH - -	5	4		
	217	-		
DONAH Paſs				
Dumrah. (See Champah Paſs) - - -	96	2		
Donah Paſs - -	5	0		
	101	2		
DUMROY. See page 8.	72	6		
DURBUNGAH. See Ammerpour - -	60	2		
DYNAPOUR Cantonments. See page 8. - -	11	4		
ENGLISH BAZAR				
Cotwally, in Biſnee road	227	0		
Engliſh Bazar - -	5	0		
	232	0		
FATTYPOUR, in Sarun				
Dudella - - - -	8	0	Ganges R.	fer.

(Fattypour continued) -	8	0		
Shitabgunge - -	3	0		
Buftee - -	6	0		
Sooteah - - -	7	0		
Amnol - -	8	6		
Fattypour - -	5	2		
	38	0		
FRINGYBAZAR				
Naraingunge, in Comillah road - - -	455	7		
Fringybazar - -	3	1	- - -	2 fer.
	459	0		
GANJAM				
Debbe Yanna, in Calcutta 3d road - -	183	2		
Neerfah - - -	2	0		
Dummoodah River -	8	2	- - -	ford
PACHETE - -	6	3		
Panchmool - -	8	6		
Tilnar - - -	9	6		
Chatna - - -	6	4		
Duidgong - -	4	0		
Raujehaut - -	9	2	Dalkifore R.	ford
Oondah - - -	8	4		
BISSUNPOUR - -	8	0		
Buccardee - -	8	5		
Mongulpatta - -	10	0	Selai R.	ford
Rufcoond - -	5	2		
Aminpour - -	9	0		
Seerfey - - -	3	2		
Ananpour - -	7	2	Nullah	ford
Currimgur - -	5	3		
MIDNAPOUR -	6	2		
Carackpour - -	5	4	Caffai R.	ford
Mutkerchoky -	5	0		
Narangur - -	8	7	Culliaghi N.	fer.
Ganjam (page 30) -	277	4		
	606	4		
By Calcutta - -	757	7		

GAREEAH Field				
Sooty, in Calcutta 1ſt road	246	4		
Gareeah - -	3	6		
	250	2		
GAYAH. See Burwa	69	2		
GHYRETTY. See Calcutta 1ſt road - -	383	3		
GOALPARAH				
RANGAMATTY, in Biſnee road - - -	401	4		
Dudekoar - -	17	0	Suncoſs R. Gourong.	fer. ford
Jugbigopa - -	21	0	Champomatty R.	fer.
Goalparah - -	5	2	Burrumpooter R.	fer.
	444	6		
GOBINGUNGE				
GORAGOT, in Chilmary road - - -	318	4		
Gobingunge - -	10	4		
	329	0		
GODAGARY				
Comrah, in Calcutta 1ſt road - - -	254	6		
Meenkoot - -	11	6	Culcully N.	ford
Godagary - -	3	0	Ganges R.	fer.
	269	4		
GOGARY. See Purneah 2d road - - -	111	4		

GOOMAH Pafs, or Gaut. See Ramgur - -	99	6		
GORAGOT. See Chilmary	318	4		
GOWGATCHY				
Hoogly - -	374	5		
Gowgatchy - -	7	2	Hoogly R.	fer.
	381	7		
GOUR				
Rajemal, in Calcutta 1ft road - - - -	209	3		
Chattry - - -	4	2	Ganges R.	fer.
Hoffainpour - -	9	3		
Habafconna Gaut, in *Gour*	8	4	Bogrutty N.	ford
	231	4		
GOW				
Arval (page 8) - -	45	0		
Belkarra - - -	6	0		
Hummidnagore -	7	2		
Gow - - -	6	4		
	64	6		
GUIDORE 1ft road. See Calcutta 2d road -	97	4		
2d road. See Chacki 2d road -	102	3		
HAJYPOUR. See page 10.	4	6		
HAJYGUNGE. See Dacca 2d road - -	406	2		

HARRIERPOUR, in Mohurbunge				
MIDNAPOUR, in Ganjam road - - -	309	5		
HARRIERPOUR (p. 71.)	66	5		
	376	2		
HENDOOAH, or Herboe. See Noony - -	176	4		
HILSAH. See Calcutta 2d road - - -	23	4		
HOOGLY. See Calcutta 1st road - - -	374	5		
HOSEEPOUR				
Moneah (page 8) -	21	2		
Cheeran - -	6	7	Ganges R.	fer.
CHUPRAH - -	7	6		
Sewan (page 68) -	37	6		
Muttcary - -	8	3		
Haryarah - -	11	4		
Hoseepour - -	4	0		
	97	4		
HURRYAL				
Dewanserai, in Calcutta 1st road - -	265	2		
Tellyah - - -	6	5		
Bahderpour - -	3	4		
Eckarygunge - -	7	6		
Murcha - - -	3	4		
Cadalcotty Gaut - -	1	6	Nullah	ford
Bauleah - - -	5	2	Ganges R.	fer.
Koppossеah - -	6	2		
	299	7		

(Hurryal continued)	299	7		
Birraldoe - -	6	3		
Pootya - - -	3	3		
NATTORE - -	10	1		
Gobinpour - -	5	0	Attri R.	fer.
Cullum - - -	6	5	Goor R. & 1 N.	fers.
Teermussundy - -	9	6		
Nowgong - -	7	0		
Hurryal - -	3	0		
	351	1		
HYDERABAD, or Soory. See Moorshedabad 2d road - - -	225	7		
JAFFIERGUNGE. See Dacca 1st road -	390	5		
JAGRENAUT. See Ganjam - - -	547	5		
JANGUIRA. See Calcutta 1st road - -	120	3		
JAULDOE. See Singboom	229	6		
JAYNAGUR. See Palamow 2d road - -	162	3		
JEHENABAD. See page 8.	110	6		
JELLASORE. See Ganjam	355	5		

JELLINGHY				
Bahderpour, in Hurryal road - - -	275	3		
Titalya - - -	6	3		
Azimgunge - -	14	5	2 Nullahs	fors.
Jellinghy - -	10	0	Culcully R.	ford
	306	3		
JELPIGORY. See Dellamcotta - - -	319	0		
JESSORE, or Moorley				
Hurrysongkor, in Dacca road - - -	321	3		
Goalgom - -	9	7		
Boladinga - -	6	0		
Buxipour - -	9	6	Comer N.	fer.
Orinaccora - -	10	2	Nullah	ford
Jennidah - -	11	7		
NULDINGAH - -	8	2	Nowgonga	ford
Nazumpour - -	9	4	Sittareeah R.	ford
MOORLEY - -	11	0	Boirub R.	fer.
	397	7		
INDOS				
Dignagur, in Calcutta 2d road - - -	259	3		
Saturya - - -	9	0	Curree N.	ford
Gogong - -	7	2		
Indos - - -	7	0	Dummoodah R.	ford
	282	5		
JOYPOUR. See Singboom	214	6		
ISLAMABAD, or Chittagong				
Hajygunge, in Dacca 2d road - - -	406	2		

(Iſlamabad continued)	406	2		
Hakeempour - -	9	4		
Rajapour - -	5	2		
Pulyculla - -	8	0	Nullah	fer.
Noorpour - - -	6	4	Ganges R. & 1 N.	fers.
ISLAMABAD (page 37. and 78) - -	161	2		
	596	6		
ISLAMPOUR. See Burwa	37	4		
ISLAMNAGUR. See Calcutta 2d road - -	78	0		
KARNOUL. See page 10	54	1		
KEERPOY				
Mongulputta, in Ganjam road - - -	273	2		
Larigunge - -	9	0	Selai R.	ford
Keerpoy - - -	9	4		
	291	6		
KINDOOA. See Dobagaut	186	7		
KISSELPOUR, or Coſſeelpour				
Palkote, in Turgah road	247	7		
Bungroo - -	2	6		
Bunnidega - -	6	6		
Palamada - -	6	0		
Beerah - -	6	0		
Sobrah - -	7	4		
Kiſſelpour - -	5	6	Sunk R.	ford
	282	5		

KISHENAGUR				
Soory, in Moorshedabad 2d road - - -	225	7		
Purunderpour - -	5	1		
Parpour - -	6	0		
Omdarra - -	7	5		
Nanore - -	8	7		
Gokure - -	8	4		
Churka - - -	6	6		
Cutwa - - -	3	4	Adji R.	ford
Bickeyhaut - -	4	0		
Beltully - - -	11	0		
Jahanagore - -	7	2		
Nuddeah - -	3	1	Nullah	ford
KISHENAGUR -	9	0	Hoogly R.	fer.
	306	5		
KOOTY. See Palamow 2d road - - -	119	3		
KOONDAH. See Palamow 3d road - -	129	7		
KYRANTY. See Dellamcotta - - -	343	2		
LETCHWAR. See Calcutta 2d road - -	84	4		
LOKOHAR. See Ammerpour - -	109	4		
LUCHMIPOUR, in Jungleterry				
Deogur, in Calcutta 2d road - -	146	0		

(Luchmipour continued)	146	0		
Chandun Nulla -	10	3	- -	ford
Cudhar - - -	4	c		
Luchmipour - -	3	4		
	163	7		
LOWYAH. See page 10	78	7		
LUCKIPOUR, in Dacca Province. See Islamabad	499	4		
LUCKIDUAR				
Dewangunge, in Coos Beyhar 2d road - -	311	7		
Saibgunge, or *Raymgunge*	11	6	Goggot R.	ford
Luckiduar (page 43) -	60	1		
	383	6		
LOHURSY Pass. See Palamow 3d road -	149	3		
LOW-COOTY				
Mowah - -	47	5		
Hadypour - -	11	0		
Monjowl - -	11	0	Bogmutty R.	fer.
Low-Cooty - -	5	6		
	75	3		
MAHRAJEGUNGE, in Purneah. See Coos Beyhar 2d road - -	251	3		
MAHMUDPOUR				
Boosnah, in Backergunge road - - -	394	7		
MAHMUDPOUR -	8	6	Burrashee R.	fer.
	403	5		

MAISSEY. See Maniahry	54	3		
MANBOOM. See Midnapour 2d road - -	263	2		
MANGEE. See Suagra	47	3		
MANJEAH, or Manjean. See Palamow 1st road	144	0		
MANIAHRY				
Daoudnagur (page 10)	25	7		
Buckrah - - -	5	5		
Jaintpour - -	5	6	Byar N.	ford
Sarra - - -	8	5		
Maissey - - -	8	4	LittleGunduckR.	ford
Madban - - -	6	0		
Chodarceah - -	10	4	Buckiah R.	ford
Jewly - - -	4	6		
Maniahry - - -	8	4	Ditto	ford
	84	1		
MANPOUR				
BETTYAH (page 10)	100	0		
Muttyah - - -	13	5		
Manpour - - -	9	0		
	122	5		
MAULDAH. See Bisnee	229	7		
MAWBELLYPOUR. See page 8 - - -	38	0		
MAJUFFERPOUR. See Turki - - -	39	3		

MEENKOOT. See Godagary - - -	266	4		
MIDNAPOUR 1st road. See Ganjam - -	309	5		
MIDNAPOUR, 2d road by Manboom				
Joypour, in Singboom Road	214	6		
Rogonautgunge - -	11	0	Cassai R.	ford
Chacultury - -	12	0		
Niagur - - -	9	3		
Juggelah - -	4	0		
Jettajoory - -	7	6		
Manboom - -	4	3		
Baroneah - -	5	6		
Aminagur - -	6	2	Cassai R. twice	fords
Muttyalla - -	5	4	Ditto	ford
Gopalpour - -	5	0	Cassai R.	ford
Gwinada - -	5	6	Ditto	ford
Roypour - - -	4	0	Ditto	ford
Bulrampour - -	10	0		
Pertapour - -	8	4	Ditto	ford
Boitau - - -	6	0	Ditto	ford
Jinjenny - -	7	2	Ditto	ford
Mohdypour - -	6	6	Ditto	ford
MIDNAPOUR -	7	6	Ditto	ford
	341	6		
MOISHPOUR. See Birkooty	222	2		
MOBOG Gaut, or Pass				
Futtypour, in Dobagaut road - - -	216	3		
Mobog Gaut - -	4	0		
	220	3		
MONEER. (See page 8)	124	3		

MONEAH. (See page 8)	21	2		
MONGHIR. See Calcutta 1st road - -	99	4		
MONGULHAUT. See Buxaduar 1st road -	358	0		
MOORSHEDABAD, or Mootyjyl, 1st road, by Terriagully. See Calcutta 1st road -	281	5		
MOORSHEDABAD, or Mootyjyl, 2d road, by Birboom				
NAGORE, in Calcutta 2d road - -	209	7		
Dulebpour Gaut -	7	5		
Soory, or Hyderabad -	8	3		
Angergurrya - -	6	2	More R.	ford
Bajetpour - -	6	0		
Telloah - -	7	1		
Boudgong - -	7	2		
Seerpour (Jillee) -	8	1		
Callyongunge - -	6	2	2 Nullahs	ford
MOORSHEDABAD -	13	5		
	280	4		
MOORLEY, or Jessore. See Jessore - -	397	7		
MOWAH				
Rajowly, in Bellya road	43	2		
Mowah - - -	4	3	Byar N.	ford
	47	5		

MUNCALGUR Pafs. The fame as Dobagaut				
MUSTAN GUR. See Silhet - - -	321	0		
NABOBGUNGE (Hoodjerapour)				
RAJEMAL, in Calcutta 1ft road - -	209	3		
Chattry - - -	4	2	Ganges R.	fer.
Hoffainpour - -	9	3		
Goreally Chuck -	6	6		
Maddapour - -	6	4	Bogrutty R.	ford
Pookareah - -	7	0		
Seebgunge - -	4	6		
Nabobgunge - -	11	0	Mahanada R.	fer.
	259	0		
NAGPOUR (Chuta). See Doefah - -	217	7		
NAGORE, or Birboom. See Calcutta, 2d road -	209	7		
NAGORBUSSY				
Mow, in Ammerpour road	20	4		
Cooty - - -	15	0		
Tafpour - - -	4	0		
Nagorbuffy - -	10	0		
	49	4		
NAGORKEEARY				
Serampour - -	148	4		
Panreedy - -	10	6	Burrakur R.	ford
	159	2		

(Nagorkeeary continued)	159	2	
Gadee-Toonree -	3	6	
* *Nagorkeeary* - -	8	6	
	171	6	
NARANGUR. See Ganjam - -	329	0	
NARANGUNGE. See Comillah - - -	455	7	
NATTORE. See Hurryal	319	6	
NAUTPOUR			
DURBUNGAH, in Ammerpour road -	60	2	
Neerah - - -	12	0	
Bowr - - -	8	0	
Jenjapour - -	8	0	
Arruah - -	7	2	
Folparas - - -	10	4	
Madumot - -	12	0	
Pirtypatty - -	12	4	
Govenpour - -	8	4	
Nautpour - -	9	0	
	148	0	
NOBUTPOUR. See page 8	139	4	
NOONY, 1st road by Monghir. See Dobagaut -	188	7	

NOONY, 2d road by Chacki Pass				
Deogur, in Calcutta 2d road	146	0		
Teernagur - -	8	1		
Jonkah - - -	6	4		
Taljarra - - -	1	0		
Burgoo - - -	7	2		
Noony - - -	7	5		
	176	4		
NORUNGAH				
Daoudnagur (page 8) -	67	1		
Dearee - -	10	4		
Ovara - - -	3	4		
Molanagur - -	5	4		
Norungah - -	4	6		
	91	3		
NOWADAH. See Calcutta 3d road - -	65	6		
NOWAPARAH, in Gongpour				
Nowadee, in Turgah road	223	0		
Guttah - - -	5	4		
Raidee - -	12	0		
Jurtulla - -	6	0	Sunk R.	ford
Kondara - -	8	0		
Kulakeera - -	10	4		
Kurrigoora - -	6	0		
Kurmdeah - -	12	0		
Beura - - -	7	4		
Nowaparah - -	14	0		
(Limit of Bahar)	304	4		
NUDDEAH. See Kishenagur	297	5		
NULDINGAH. See Jessore	377	3		

NULSHI Imaumpour. See Dacca 3d road -	369	1		
OKERAH, or Seergur. See Calcutta 3d road -	223	4		
OLYAPOUR				
RUNGPOUR, in Bisnee road - - -	334	5		
Baminycula - -	11	5	Nullah	ford
Teetari - - -	5	2		
Olyepour - - -	6	2	Teesta N.	fer.
	357	6		
OUDANULLA. See Calcutta 1st road -	215	7		
PACHETE. See Ganjam	199	7		
PALGUNGE. See Singboom - - -	157	1		
PALAMOW, 1st road				
Daoudnagur (page 8) -	67	1		
Pipra Gur - -	11	0		
Cadgery - -	10	4		
Momaiah - -	9	4		
Kadzurim - -	6	4		
Dongwar - -	8	0		
Diowry - - -	8	6		
Pansah - -	6	6		
Morubba - - -	9	0		
Manjeah - -	7	0		
* *Bisrampour* - -	14	0		
	158	1		

(Palamow 1st road continued)	158	1	
* Sidra - - -	17	0	
* *Jaynagur* - - -	15	0	
* *PALAMOW* - -	13	0	
	203	1	
PALAMOW, 2d road by Sheergotty, and Monatoo Pass - -			
Gayah, in Burwa Road	69	2	
Buttah - - -	6	3	
Colera - - -	5	0	
Gouah - - -	6	6	
Sheergotty - -	10	0	
Dumroy - - -	7	4	
Ecmangunge - -	7	0	
Kooty - - -	7	4	
* Dumeerbary - -	17	0	
Monatoo Pass - -	5	0	
* Terussee - - -	9	0	
* *Jaynagur* - -	11	0	
* *Palamow* - -	13	0	
	174	3	
PALAMOW 3d road, by Koonda and Lohursey Pass			
Sheergotty, as before	97	3	
Sunpoora - -	7	0	
* Dahree - -	15	0	
* *Koonda* - -	10	4	
Dewar - - -	9	0	
Lohursey Pass - -	10	4	
* *Jaynagur* - -	18	0	
PALAMOW - -	13	0	
	180	3	
PALCOTE. See Turgah	247	7	

PATCHWARRY. See Birkooty - -	204	0		
PATCOOM. See Singboom	260	1		
PAUNRAW. See Calcutta 3d road - -	186	3		
PERSAH				
BETTYAH (page 10) -	100	0		
Persah (page 59) -	50	0		
	150	0		
PLASSEY. See Calcutta 1st road -	307	6		
POINTY. See Coos Beyhar 2d road - -	173	2		
POLLAY				
Sadabad, (page 8) -	30	0		
Pollay - -	6	6		
	36	6		
POOKAREEAH Purgunnah, in Raujeshy				
Nulshi, in Dacca 3d road	369	1		
Dubya Gaut - -	2	6	Joobnee R.	fer.
Gopaulgunge - -	5	0	2 Nullahs	{ fer. ford
Moodupour Cutcherry -	6	0	Bunse R.	ford
	3[illegible]2	[illegible]		
PUBNA-NAZIRPOUR. See Dacca 1st road	347	5		

PUCCULOE. See Dacca 3d road -	399	3		
PURNEAH, 1st road by Caragola. See Coos Beyhar 2d road - -	212	7		
PURNEAH, 2d road by Bowanypour				
MONGHIR, in Calcutta 1st road - -	99	4		
Gogary - -	12	0	Ganges R.	fer.
Seral - - -	12	0		
Duryah Gaut -	2	0	Gogary R.	fer.
Loaky - - -	14	0		
Mugdumpour -	8	0		
Bowanypour -	8	4		
Etarry Gaut - -	5	4	Cosah R.	fer.
Baraillah - -	4	0		
Sahebgunge - -	8	5		
Old Coosey River -	3	5	- - -	ford
PURNEAH - -	5	0		
	182	6		
PURNEAH, 3d road by Durbungah				
DURBUNGAH, in Ammerpour Road -	60	2		
Neerah - - -	12	0		
Bowr - - -	8	0		
Jenjapour - -	8	0		
Maddipour - -	11	0		
Carrary - -	3	4		
Pursaummah - -	15	0		
Jowreah - -	7	4		
Sangeasatoun - -	10	2		
Helvanagur, or *Hellomargunge* - -	7	2		
	142	6		

(Purneah, 3d road continued)	142	6		
Mulygunge -	8	4		
Bernagur - -	11	0		
Cundwah Gaut -	13	0	Coosy R.	fer.
Old Coosy River -	11	2	- - -	ford
PURNEAH - -	5	2		
	191	6		
PURRUAH. See Dinagepour	237	1		
RAJEMAL. See Calcutta 1st road - -	209	3		
RAJABARRY. See Islamabad - - -	459	4		
RAJOWLY. See Ramgur	83	1		
RAJEGUNGE. The same as Dinagepour -	286	3		
RAMGUR				
Nowadah, in Calcutta 3d road - - -	65	6		
Burdhoo, or Bertha -	3	0		
Rajowly - - -	14	0		
* Singur - - -	7	4		
* *Goomah* Gaut - -	9	4		
Goomah Fort - -	6	4		
* Purki - - -	13	0		
* Etchauk - -	13	0	Burrakur R.	ford
* *Muckundgunge* -	15	0		
* *Andra-Jerba* Pass -	14	0		
* *RAMGUR* - -	17	0		
	178	2		

RANGAMATTY. See Bisnee - -	401	4	
RANYPOOKRA Gaut. See Singboom - -	187	0	
RAYMGUNGE. The same as Saibgunge. See Luckiduar - - -	323	5	
ROGONATPOUR			
PACHETE, in Ganjam road - - -	199	7	
ROGONATPOUR -	8	1	
	208	0	
ROONAY. See Suryah 2d road - - -	142	6	
ROTA, or Ratta Pass			
Mellypour, in Chacki 2d road - - -	92	0	
Pandoo - - -	5	3	
Calagong - -	8	2	
Koomree - -	7	5	
Usslah - - -	7	0	
Rangah - - -	5	4	
Kewsor - - -	5	6	
Rota Pass - -	2	3	
	133	7	
ROTAS GUR			
Durnyhaut (page 8)	80	2	
Dander - - -	8	4	
	88	6	

(Rotas Gur continued)	88	6		
Thilouta - - -	10	4		
Callyampour - -	12	2		
ROTAS GUR - -	7	0	Nullah	ford
	118	2		
ROW. See Delour Gaut, 2d road - - -	71	1		
RUNGPOUR 1st road. See Bisnee - - -	335	4		
RUNGPOUR 2d road, by Dinagepour				
DINAGEPOUR -	286	3		
Sumdeah - -	11	5	Attri R.	fer.
Poolbarry - -	12	3	2 Nullahs	ford
Pookareeah - -	7	5	Nullah	ford
Kissunagur - -	8	2	2 Nullahs	ford
Mullung - -	6	0		
RUNGPOUR - -	7	0		
	339	2		
SAIBGUNGE Cantonments. See Luckiduar	323	5		
SANASHYGOTTA				
Titalya, in Dellamcotta road - - -	291	3		
Sanashygotta - -	9	4		
	300	7		
SARHAUT. See Calcutta 2d road - -	169	4		
SASERAM (page 8) -	93	3		

SEEBGUNGE, in Raujeſhy. See Silhet - -	314	6		
SEEDLEY *DURBUNGAH*, in Ammerpour road - -	60	2		
Seedley (page 66) -	93	2		
	153	4		
SEERPOUR, in Mahmanſhy. See Dacca 3d road -	338	7		
SEERGUR, or Okera. See Calcutta 3d road -	223	4		
SERRIS. See Cotumbah	88	1		
SERAMPOUR. See Calcutta 3d road -	148	4		
SEWAN, or Allygunge. See Hoſeepour -	73	4		
SHILBERIS, the ſame as *Buygurah*. See Dacca 3d road - - -	324	7		
SHEERGOTTY. See Palamow 3d road -	97	3		
SHEIKPOUR. See Balguda 2d road - -	67	0		

SICLYGULLY. See Calcutta 1st road - -	190	0		
SILLEE				
Jauldoe, in Singboom road	229	6		
Sillee - - -	12	0		
	241	6		
SINGHYAH. See page 10	17	4		
SILHET				
Etacola, in Dacca 3d road	302	3		
Baumundiggy - -	2	7		
Seebgunge - -	9	4	Currattya R.	ford
Munstangur - -	6	2		
Bowanyhaut - -	1	7	Ditto	ford
Joyboka - - -	8	2		
Duregahatty - -	6	0	Nullah	ford
Comerpara - -	4	4		
Nokeela - - -	3	2	Monaash R.	fer.
Golabary - -	7	4	Nullah	ford
Hajypour - -	9	0	Jenni R.	ford
Buzrapour - -	6	2		
Pykerhaut - -	10	6	Nullah	ford
Ectal - - -	5	3		
Bygonbary - -	11	2		
Cassergunge - -	9	3	Burrumpooter R.	fer.
Bokinagur - -	10	2	2 Nullahs	ford
Chumaroola - -	10	6	1 ditto	ford
Murchagunge - -	9	2	1 ditto	ford
Junglebary - -	9	0		
Panchcownya - -	11	0	Nullah	fer.
Ectna - - -	7	1	Dunnu and Bolee Rs.	fers.
Azmerigunge - -	10	0	Lamakerra, & Megna Rivers	fers.
Banniachung - -	8	1		
Connipour - -	9	4		
	489	3		

Silhet continued)	489	3		
Agnah - - -	5	2	Nullah	ford
* Cattyah - - -	11	0		
* Bunbaug - -	10	0	Buſſya R.	ford
* *SILHET* - -	9	2	Soormah R.	fer.
	524	7		
SINGBOOM				
Serampour, in Calcutta 3d road - - -	148	4		
Palgunge - -	8	5	Burrakur R.	ford
Mudjelaidy - -	8	2		
Palgunge Paſs - -	2	1		
Niahgur - -	15	0		
Rannypookra Gaut -	4	4	Dummoodah R.	ford
Naranpour - -	11	6		
Ringaudee - -	8	0		
Jeypour - - -	8	0		
Bauguncooda - -	8	0	Caſſai R.	ford
Jauldoe - - -	7	0		
Ordonnah - -	8	0		
Burſoot - -	5	7		
Jilling - - -	4	4		
Patcoom - - -	12	0		
* *SINGBOOM*, by Banſa Paſs	26	0		
	286	1		
SOOTY. See Calcutta 1ſt road - - -	246	4		
SOORY, or Hyderabad. See Moorſhedabad 2d road	225	7		
SUAGRA				
CHUPRAH, in Hoſeepour road - - -	35	7		
Gudena - -	5	2		
	41	1		

(Suagra continued)	41	1		
Mangee - - -	6	2		
Suagra (page 73) -	46	1		
	93	4		
SULTANABAD. The same as Birkooty				
SURYA 1st road. See Calcutta 2d road -	157	6		
SURYA 2d road				
Chacki, in Calcutta 2d road - - -	125	4		
Poonassy - -	9	2		
Roonay - - -	8	0		
Surya - - -	12	1		
	154	7		
SUTALURY				
Madapassa, in Backergunge road - - -	480	5		
Mogossy - -	7	4	2 Nullahs	fer.
Sutalury - - -	5	0	1 ditto	fer.
	493	1		
TAUJEPOUR, in Purneah				
PURNEAH - -	182	6		
Chickneeah - -	4	4		
Durghyagunge - -	7	4	Dubelly R.	ford
Nabobgunge - -	6	6		
Hidgeah - -	2	3	Mahanada R.	ford
Rampour - -	7	4	Sudanny R.	ford
Taujepour - -	9	5	Nagore R.	ford
	221	0		
TARRAPOUR. See Bircooty - - -	124	6		

TERRIAGULLY. See Calcutta 1ſt road -	177	2
TICKARRY		
Ruſtangunge (page 8)	16	0
Fetwas - - -	9	0
Futtyapour - -	5	4
Kemjar - - -	9	4
Dararah - -	5	3
Cholaky - - -	7	3
Tickarry - -	7	0
	59	6
TIKOO, or TIKOO MONATOO. See Burwa	175	3
TIPERAH, or Comillah. See Comillah -	505	6
TISSIAH Paſs		
Odeygunge, in Burwa Road	161	5
Toree - - -	2	6
Chundſah - -	5	2
Sulgee - - -	8	6
Tiſſiah - -	3	0
Ditto Paſs - -	2	0
	183	3
TOMAR, or Tamar		
Sillee - - -	241	6
* *Tomar* - - -	12	0
	253	6
TOREE. See Tiſſiah	165	3

TUREE, or Tuer				
Deogur, in Calcutta 2d road	146	0		
Turee - - -	8	1		
	154	1		
TURKI				
HAJYPOUR - -	4	6	Ganges R.	fer.
Seraha - - -	8	4		
Byar Nullah - -	9	0	- -	ford
Fukoly Bridge -	3	6		
Cundupatty - -	2	5	Nuna N.	ford
Lodara - -	6	0		
Majufferpour - -	4	6	LittleGunduckR	ford
Mustasaggee - -	10	0		
Turki - -	5	6		
	55	1		
TURGAH, in Chuta Nagpour				
Bootee, in Burwah Road	198	7		
Nudeah - - -	4	0		
Burcahdy - -	7	2		
Sebrajepour - -	4	0		
Nowadee - -	7	4		
Korah - -	6	2		
Beerndah - -	5	4		
Ormah - - -	8	0		
Palcote - - -	5	4		
Nautpour - -	3	4		
Morung - -	3	4		
Lurbah - - -	6	4		
Tyserra - -	9	4		
Sillingah - -	8	0		
Turgah - -	14	0		
	291	7		

TABLES OF ROADS,

FROM

D A C C A,

TO ALL THE PRINCIPAL PLACES IN

BENGAL AND BAHAR.

Expreſſing the Length of the Stages, and the Number and Situation of the Fords and Ferries.

TABLES OF ROADS,

From DACCA, to all the principal Places in BENGAL and BAHAR.

Names of Places.	distances in Miles and Furl.		Rivers and Nullahs to be crossed.	ford or ferry.
AHMIRABADS Purgunnah				
Chandergunge, in Islamabad 2d road -	86	7		
Buzrah Cutchery -	6	2		
	93	1		
AMBOOAH. See Burdwan 2d road - -	161	1		
AMMERPOUR, in Morung				
PURNEAH - -	283	3		
AMMERPOUR (page 1)	75	7		
	359	2		
ATTYAH. See Mauldah 2d road - -	57	6		
AZMERIGUNGE, 1st road by Nursingdee				
Lacki (page 69) -	81	0		
Betalung - -	12	6	Brack R.	fer.
Azmerigunge - -	8	2		
	102	0		

AZMERIGUNGE, 2d road by Junglebary				
Junglebary (page 42)	70	0		
Panchcownya - -	11	0	Nullah	fer.
Eeteneah - -	7	1	Dunnuh & Bolee R.	fer.
Azmerigunge - -	10	0	Lammakerra & Megna R.	fer.
	98	1		
BACKERGUNGE				
Pattergotta - -	6	0	Boorygonga & Dollaserry Rs.	fer.
Surajady - -	5	0		
Duchinchargong -	4	3		
Dunconya - -	5	7	Nullah	ford
Nullua - - -	6	6		
Buderashon - -	7	0	Ganges R.	fer.
Hobibgunge - -	8	0	3 Nullahs	1 fer. 2 ford
Backergunge (page 5) -	56	4		
	99	4		
BAHAR. See Patna 2d road	401	3		
BALASORE. See Ganjam	320	5		
BALLITUNGY. See Cutwa	155	3		
BAMINY				
Madapassa, in Backergunge road - - - -	83	2		
Mogossy - - -	7	4	2 Nullahs	ford
Sutalury - - -	5	0		
Moddypour - -	0	4	Domudar R.	fer.
	96	2		

(Baminy continued) -	96	2		
* Charcolly - -	22	0	2 Nullahs	fer.
* *Baminy* - - -	13	0		
	131	2		
BANGAH				
Sunerampour, in meri-gunge 1st road -	56	1		
Bangah (page 6) -	137	3		
	193	4		
BANNIACHUNG. See Silhet 2d road -	100	6		
BAULEAH. See Purneah	152	0		
BAZETPOUR, or Bajit-pour Aurung				
Dulcheddy, in Azmeri-gunge 2d road -	38	6		
Noylacote - -	9	0		
Bazetpour - -	11	0	Burrampooter R.	fer.
	58	6		
BEJURAH				
Hurringber, in Bangah road - -	73	4		
Bejurah - -	5	0		
	78	4		
BELCUCHY. See Maul-dah 2d road -	76	2		
BENARES, 1st road by Patna				
Pattergotta - -	6	0	{ Boorygonga & Dollaserry Rs }	fer.

(Benares 1ſt road, continued)	6	0		
Seckinagur - -	8	4	Nullah	fer.
Churan - -	2	4	2 Ditto	fer.
Bandura - -	9	2	Iſſamutty R.	fer.
Burruacally - -	3	1		
Jattrapour - -	8	0	Surramutty R.	ford
Jeetka - - -	5	2		
Chanpara - -	6	7	Cantabotey R.	fer.
Jaffiergunge - -	6	3		
Ruttungunge - -	10	0	2 Rivers	fer.
Nazagunge - -	8	4		
Sujanagur - -	12	4		
Pubna - - -	12	0	Arti R.	fer.
Comitpour - -	6	2		
Shawpour - -	5	6	Ganges R.	fer.
Damadure - -	3	6		
Hurryſongkor -	10	4		
Culcully Termonee -	11	4	Jellinghee R.	ford
Azimgunge - -	8	2		
Dultabazar - -	11	6		
Balloo - -	2	5	Nullah	fer.
MOORSHEDABAD (*Mootyjyl*) - -	5	5		
PATNA (page 55) -	281	5		
BENARES (page 8) -	165	4		
	512	0		
(BENARES 2d road, by Birboom				
MOORSHEDABAD, as before - -	164	7		
Iſlamnagur (page 57)	202	4		
Rypour - -	12	0		
Curree - -	6	4		
Bertha, or Burdhoo -	6	6		
BENARES (page 9)	189	0		
	581	5		
BERMYAH				
Tizgong - -	5	0		

(Bermyah continued) -	5	0		
Tunghy Bridge -	8	4		
Judookpour - -	9	3		
Nallyatangy - -	9	3	2 Nullahs	ford
Garrarawn - -	9	7	Nullah	ford
Bermyah - -	3	4		
	45	5		

BETTYAH				
PATNA, in Benares 1st road	446	4		
BETTYAH (page 10)	100	0		
	546	4		

BEYHAR, or Coos-Beyhar. See Buxaduar -	243	2		

BIRBOOM, or Nagore. See Benares 2d road -	235	4		

BISSUNPOUR				
Bungong, in Calcutta Road	136	6		
Sirinagur - -	9	6		
Sutagotchy - -	13	4		
Niaſerai - - -	6	0	Hoogly R.	fer.
Purruah - -	8	3	Nullah	ford
Böenchee - -	5	1		
Chautkundy - -	5	7		
Burſool - -	12	4		
BURDWAN - -	7	6		
Moor - - -	7	0	Dummooda R.	ford
Dubrajehaut - -	6	4		
Indos - - -	4	1		
Balſee - - -	5	6		
Gapalnagur - -	8	5	Dalkiſor R.	ford
BISSUNPOUR -	7	5		
	245	2		

BISNEE				
PUCCULOE, in Mauldah 2d road -	49	4		
Batcoora - -	9	2		
Booketah Aurung -	3	4		
Hummidpour - -	8	0		
Chamtarra - -	6	2		
Moodupcur (*Pookarya*)	10	1	Bunse R.	ford
Bowlah - - -	10	1	Ditto	ford
Naranpour - -	7	3	Ditto twice	fords
Hajypour - -	6	3	Jenni R.	ford
Shazadpour - -	7	0		
Dewangunge - -	14	5	3 Nullahs	fords
Hurchundy - -	8	4		
Mobagunge - -	7	2		
Chilmary - -	6	7	Nullah	ford
Callygunge - -	9	4	Nullah	ford
Olyapour - - -	10	6	Teesta N.	ford
Bisnee (page 12) -	129	3		
	304	3		
BITTREBUND Purgannah (Paradanga Cutcherry)				
Deenhottah, in Bisnee road	196	4		
Paradanga - -	4	6	Nullah	ford
	201	2		
BOGWANGOLA. See Meenkoot - -	167	7		
BOGLIPOUR. See Benares 1st road - -	309	2		
BOKINAGUR, in Momanfing. See Susung -	90	1		
BOOSNAH. See Burdwan 2d road - -	63	0		

BOWAL				
Tizgong - -	5	0		
Tunghy Bridge -	8	4		
Bowal - - -	7	3	2 Nullahs	{ 1 fer. 1 for.
	20	-		
BOWANIGUNGE. See Mauldah 2d road	148	4		
BUDDAUL				
Eetacola, in Purneah 2d road - -	146	4		
Jamaulgunge - -	6	6	Nullah	ford
Saumgunge - -	7	6	Jubuna N.	ford
Buddaul - -	4	4		
	165	4		
BUGGURA. (Cutcherry of Shilberis) See Purneah 2d road -	124	2		
BULLOOAH				
Luckipour, in Islamabad 1st road - -	72	0		
Bullooah - - -	10	2	Nullah	fer.
	82	2		
BURDWAN 1st road. See Bissunpour - -	205	5		
BURDWAN 2d road, by Kishenagur				
Gopalpour, in Calcutta Road - - -	55	2		

(Burdwan 2d road, continued)	55	2		
Boosnah - -	7	6		
Baboocally - -	4	0	Burrashee R.	fer.
Magrah - -	9	1	Nowgonga R.	fer.
Ramnagur - -	7	1		
Jennidah - -	11	1		
Gopalpour - -	10	4	Mussaw N.	ford
Dyatty - - -	8	3		
Dowlatgunge - -	6	1	Cobbaduck R.	ford
Muttyary - -	4	0		
Sibnibas - -	4	2	Issamot R.	fer.
Ilaburrya - -	8	0		
KISHENAGUR -	5	2		
Dignagur - -	6	0		
Santipour - -	8	3		
Ambooah - -	5	7	Hoogly R.	fer.
Culna - - -	2	6		
Sacheroy haut -	5	7		
San'gutchy - -	6	2		
Konchote - -	7	0		
Bykuntpour - -	7	2	Nullah	ford
BURDWAN - -	4	4		
	194	6		
BURHAMPOUR Cantonment				
Balloo, in Benares 1st road	159	2		
Burhampour - -	7	4		
	166	6		
BURGANCOOTY				
Gobirgunge, in Buxaduar road - -	149	2		
Burgancooty - -	2	0		
	151	2		
BUXAR				
PATNA - -	446	4		
Buxar (page 8) -	85	1		
	531	5		

BUXIGUNGE. See Purneah 2d road - -	167	0		
BUXIPOUR (in Mahmud-shi). See Cutwa	113	1		
BUXADUAR				
Buggurah, in Purneah 2d road - -	124	2		
Mustangur - -	7	6		
Seebgunge - -	6	2	Nullah	ford
Gobingunge - -	11	0	Currattya R.	ford
Palasbery - -	11	0		
Haatybunder - -	7	4	Ankera N.	ford
Burradirga - -	9	4		
Mettypokre - -	4	5		
Dumdumma - -	6	3		
RUNGPOUR - -	3	3	Goggot R.	fer.
Buxaduar (page 16) -	95	0		
	286	5		
BYGONBARY. See Seerpour Duscownya -	100	5		
CALCUTTA				
Pattergotta - -	6	0	Boorygonga & Dollaserry R.	fer.
Churan - - -	11	0	3 Nullahs	fer.
Nabobgunge - -	6	0		
Mynehaut - -	7	2	Issamutty R.	fer.
Nurilapour - -	3	0		
Hajygunge - -	7	0	Ganges R. & a Nullah	fers.
Furridpour - -	6	2		
Gopalpour - -	8	6		
Jaynagur - -	7	0	Comer N.	fer.
MAHMUDPOUR -	7	3	Burrashee R.	fer.
	69	5		

(Calcutta continued) -	69	5		
Nobutta - -	7	4		
Gunagotta - -	7	6	Nowgonga R.	fer.
Docallee - -	8	6	Sittarya R.	fer.
Rajapour - -	4	2	Ditto	fer.
Neelgunge - -	5	4		
MOORLEY, or *JESSORE*	2	0	Boyrub R.	fer.
Jingergutcba - -	7	7	Nullah	ford
Jadopour - -	7	0	Cobaduck R.	fer.
Porabary - -	5	6	Nullah	fer.
Bungong - - -	5	6	2 do. & Issamutty R	fers.
Chanpara - -	6	0		
Mullickpour - -	6	5		
Janapole - - -	4	3	Jubuna N.	ford
Jawberrya - -	3	7		
Dottapugrey - -	7	5		
Barajet - - -	5	6		
Dumdum - -	7	4		
CALCUTTA Old Fort	6	0		
	179	4		
CALCUTTA 2d road, direct to Hajygunge				
Tagoorpour - -	5	4	Boorygonga R.	fer.
Churan - - -	9	0	Dollaserry, Issamuttty, & 1 Nullah	fer.
CALCUTTA, as before	162	4		
	177	0		
CALLYAJURY				
Azmerigunge - -	98	1		
Moradpour - -	5	6	Megna R.	fer.
Callyajury - -	5	7	Bolee R.	fer.
	109	6		
CARAGOLA				
Nabobgunge, in Purneah 1st road - -	18[illegible]	6		
Caragola - - -	14	3		
	196	1		

CASSIMPOUR. See Pattergotta in Attyah -	22	7		
CAULEAH, in Burbazzoo				
Nulſbi, in Purneah 2d road	79	6		
Cauleah - - -	5	4	Coni & Iſſamutty R	fer.
	85	2		
CAUGMAHRY				
Suntoſh, in Maulda 2d road	62	0		
Caugmahry - -	2	0		
	64	0		
CHANDPOUR				
Mutlupgunge, in Iſlamabad road - -	40	6		
Chandpour - -	9	6		
	50	4		
CHANDERNAGORE				
Mullickpour, in Calcutta Road - - -	144	3		
Chuprah - - -	7	5		
Moſundah - -	5	0		
Chinſurah - -	9	0	Hoogly R.	fer.
Chandernagore - -	2	6		
	168	6		
CHACKI, or Fort Haſtings. See Benares 2d road	319	7		
CHATMOL				
Pubna, in Purneah 1ſt road	98	7		
Syngpine - -	10	6	Arti R.	fer.
Chatmol - -	9	4	Attri R.	ford
	110	1		

CHARCOLLY. See Baminy	118	2		
CHINSURAH. See Chandernagore - -	166	0		
CHILMARY. See Biſnee	154	6		
CHICHACOTTA. See Buxaduar - -	261	6		
CHITTIGONG. The ſame as Iſlamabad - -	151	7		
CHURAN. See Calcutta	17	0		
CHUPRAH				
Moneab, in Benares 1ſt road	467	6		
Cheeran - - -	6	7	Ganges R.	fer.
CHUPRAH - -	7	6		
	482	3		
CHUNARGUR				
Mogulſerai, in Benares 2d road - - -	572	7		
Chunargur - -	18	0		
	590	7		
COLINDA. See Iſlamabad 1ſt road - -	101	6		
COMERCALLY. See Moorſhedabad 2d road	93	1		

COMILLAH. See Kundal	59	2		
CONSUMAHGUNGE				
Sumdeah, in Purneah 2d road - - -	191	2		
Tultully - -	9	0		
Rannyhaut - -	10	4		
Consumahgunge - -	11	6		
	222	4		
COORSAH				
Saftybary, in Buxaduar Road - - -	205	4		
Quoilagot - -	6	3	Durla R.	fer.
Coorsah - - -	6	6	Neelcomer R.	fer.
	218	5		
COSSIMBUZAR 1st road				
Balloo, in Benares 1st road	159	2		
COSSIMBUZAR -	5	5		
	164	7		
COSSIMBUZAR 2d road, by Hajygunge				
Balloo in Moorshedabad 2d road - - -	159	2		
COSSIMBUZAR - -	5	5		
	164	7		
COSSIDYA. See Islamabad 1st road - -	110	6		
CULNA, in Burdwan. See Burdwan 2d road	163	7		

CULNA, in Jeſſore				
MAHMUDPOUR, in Calcutta Road - -	69	5		
Bongong - -	5	6	3 Nullahs	ford
Rajapour - - -	7	0	Nowgonga R.	fer.
Goracally - -	3	4	Sittarya R.	fer.
Samrool - - -	5	4		
Suderapour - -	7	2		
Subnara - - -	6	6	Nullah	fer.
Samgunge - -	6	6	Boirub R.	fer.
Culna - - -	8	4	Ditto	fer.
	120	5		
CUDWAH				
Burcumptah, in Kundal Road - - -	47	7		
Cudwah - - -	10	0		
	57	7		
CURYGONG. See Biſnee	188	6		
CURRUCKDEA				
Chacki, in Benares 2d road	319	7		
Nowadah - -	5	0		
Burwahdee - -	5	4		
Curruckdeah - -	6	4		
	336	7		
CURRYBARRY Purgannah. It lies on the Eaſt ſide of the Burrampooter River, oppoſite Chilmary.				
CUSTEE. See Mooiſhedabad 2d road - -	103	5		

CUTWA				
Comercally, in Moorsheda-bad 2d road - -	93	1		
Aulumpour - -	10	6	Gorroy N.	ford
Buxipour - - -	9	2	Comer N.	ford
Bagawdy - - -	9	0	Ditto, twice	ford
Banchbury - -	6	4	2 Nullahs	ford
Oujalpour - -	8	6	Boyrub N.	ford
Bettay - - -	5	4		
Buxypour - -	8	6	2 Nullahs	ford
Bal'ytunghy - -	3	6	Jellinghy R.	ford
Plassey - - -	12	6		
Anutpour - -	6	2		
Cutwa - - -	6	0	Cossimbuzar R.	ford
	180	3		
CUTTACK. See Ganjam	427	1		
DAOUDCANDY. See Kundal - -	26	3		
DAOUDNAGUR. See Benares 2d road -	483	2		
DARRA, in Jungleterry				
Sabaut, in Benares 2d road	275	7		
Gurgurree - -	10	2		
Burgoo - - -	9	6		
Kindooah - - -	8	4		
Darra - - -	15	2		
	319	5		
DEOGUR, or Deugur. See Benares 2d road -	299	3		

DELLAMCOTTA, in Bootan				
RUNGPOUR, in Buxaduar Road - - -	191	5		
Little Jaffiergunge -	8	4		
Ameergunge - -	5	4		
Sunagur - - -	7	6	Goggot R.	ford
Calpaany - - -	9	4	Ditto	ford
Cheerabeja - -	8	0	Ditto	ford
Subungunge - -	9	2	Ditto	ford
Saibgunge, or *Raymgunge*	4	6		
Dellamcotta (page 26) -	63	2		
	310	1		
DEWANGUNGE (in Patladah). See Bisnee -	132	1		
DINAGEPOUR. See Purneah 2d road - -	202	7		
DOESAH, or Chuta Nagpour				
NAGORE, in Benares 2d road - - -	235	4		
Imumgur Gaut - -	5	1		
Lacaracoonda - -	5	5		
Petrabad (page 90) -	105	2		
DOESAH (page 16) -	85	1		
	436	5		
DULYA-GUBINDPOUR				
Gorypassah, in Backergunge road - -	92	0		
Surajabads - -	6	2	Nullah	fer.
Gubindpour - -	9	5	Amtoly N.	fer.
Dulya - - -	1	6	Sunacally R.	fer.
	109	5		

DUMROY. See Mauldah 2d road - - -	25	3		
DURBUNGAH				
MONGHIR, in Benares 1st road - - -	347	0		
Bellyah - - -	9	6	Ganges R.	fer.
Low-Cooty - -	11	0	Bogmutty R.	fer.
Monjowl - -	5	6		
Sacrowly - -	6	4		
Barrcapour - -	6	1		
DURBUNGAH (page 66)	36	2		
	422	3		
DYNAPOUR Cantonments. See Benares 1st road	458	0		
ENGLISH BAZAR. See Purneah 1st road -	216	1		
FRINGYBAZAR. See Mendigunge - -	12	4		
GANJAM				
CALCUTTA - -	179	4		
Ganjam (page 29) -	357	5		
	537	1		
GAYAH. See Benares 2d road - - -	435	6		
GAREEAH Field				
Comrah, in Benares 1st road	191	6		
Gareeah field - -	6	6	Cossimbuzar R.	ford
	198	4		

GENTIAH				
SILHET - -	145	6		
GENTIAH (page 31) -	24	4		
	170	2		
GOALPARAH				
RANGAMATTY, in Bifnee Road - -	232	3		
Goalparah (page 32) -	43	2		
	275	5		
GOBINGUNGE. See Buxaduar - -	149	2		
GODAGARY. See Purneah 1ft road - -	173	1		
GOPALGUNGE				
Hajygunge, in Calcutta Road - - -	40	2		
Hakeempour - -	9	4		
Tingorcally - -	13	4	Comer N.	ford
Muxoodpour - -	2	0		
Coyrah - - -	7	6		
Kolna - - -	6	0	Mudamutty R.	fer.
Gopalgunge (page 32) -	17	4		
	96	4		
GORAGOT				
Seebgunge, in Buxaduar Road - - -	138	2		
Gujeah - - -	2	0		
Omlitulla - -	4	3		
GORAGOT - -	10	3		
	155	0		

GOUR Ruins				
Nabobgunge, in Purneah 1st road - -	181	6		
Habaſconna Gaut, in *Gour* (page 33) - -	27	0		
	208	6		
GOTTAUL. See Keerpoy	222	5		
GUIDORE. See Benares 2d road - -	347	7		
GURNADY. See Backergunge - - -	64	6		
GUZGOTTA				
RUNGPOUR, in Buxaduar Road - -	191	5		
Guzgotta - -	7	4		
	199	1		
GWAHREE				
KISHENAGUR, in Burdwan 2d road - -	140	7		
Gwahree - - -	2	0		
	142	7		
HAJYGUNGE. See Calcutta 1st road - -	40	2		
HAJYPOUR				
PATNA, in Benares 1st road - - -	446	4		
HAJYPOUR - -	4	6	Ganges R.	fer.
	451	2		

HOBIBGUNGE (in Dacca). See Backergunge -	43	0		
HOBIBGUNGE (in Torroff)				
Sujatpour, in Silhet 2d road	88	5		
Hobibgunge - -	8	1		
	96	6		
HOBITNAGUR				
Sagordee, in Azmerigunge 2d road - -	48	2		
Agarafondu - -	3	0	Burrampooter R.	fer.
Hobitnagur - -	14	2		
	65	4		
HOOGLY				
Mofundah, in Chandernagore Road - -	157	0		
HOOGLY - -	9	2	Hoogly R.	fer.
	166	2		
HURRYAL				
Dowlatpour, in Mauldah 2d road - -	83	3		
Ghyhutta - - -	8	4	Foolju R.	fer.
Hurryal - -	9	6		
	101	5		
HYDERABAD, or Soory. See Benares 2d road -	219	4		
JAFFIERGUNGE. See Benares 1ft road -	55	7		
JAGRENAUT. See Ganjam	478	2		

Place	Miles	Furl.	Rivers	
JALALGUNGE				
Burradirgah, in Buxaduar Road - - -	177	2		
Jalalgunge - -	8	0		
	185	2		
JANGUIRA. See Benares 1st road - -	326	1		
JARBARRY				
Consumalgunge -	222	4		
Jarbarry - -	7	6	Teesta R.	fer.
	230	2		
JAYNAGUR. See Calcutta	62	2		
JELLINGHY				
Hurrysongkor, in Benares 1st road - -	125	1		
Mayscunda - - -	4	6	Comer N.	ford
Jellinghy - -	8	0	Jelinghee R.	ford.
	137	7		
JELLASORE. See Ganjam	286	2		
JELPIGORY				
Saibgunge, in Dellamcotta road - - -	244	7		
Baccallyhaut - -	12	5	Goggot	ford
Jelpigory - -	6	7	Teesta R.	fer.
	264	3		
JENNIDAH. See Burdwan 2d road - -	94	3		

JESSORE, or Moorley. See Calcutta - -	105	4		
INDOS. See Biſſunpour	218	2		
INCHACOLUS. See Punduah - - -	149	4		
JOOGDYA				
Colinda, in Iſlamabad 1ſt road - -	101	6		
Joogdya - -	8	4		
	110	2		
JUGHIGOPA. See Goalparah - - -	270	3		
JUNGLEBARY. See Azmerigunge 2d road	70	0		
ISLAMABAD, or Chittagong 1ſt road by Luckipour				
Futtulah - - -	6	5	2 Nullahs	fer.
Naraingunge - -	2	6		
Gudjaleeah - -	7	2	- - -	3 fer.
Allynyah - -	9	0	2 Nullahs and Megna	fer.
Sujatpour - -	9	1	Nullah	ford
Mutlupgunge - -	6	0	Gomut R.	fer.
Mahabutpour - -	8	6		
Baggrah - -	4	2		
Rampour - -	9	0		
	62	6		

(Islamabad continued) -	62	6		
Luckipour - -	9	2	Dackitya R.	fer.
ISLAMABAD (page 37 and 78)	97	3		
	169	3		
ISLAMABAD, 2d road by Mahmud-Allyhaut. See page 38 - -	151	7		
KEERPOY				
Omptah, in Midnapour 1st road - - -	202	6		
Keerpoy (page 18) -	29	5		
	232	3		
KISHENAGUR. See Burdwan 2d road -	140	7		
KUNDAL				
Allynyah, in Islamabad Road - - -	25	5		
Dasudcandy - -	0	6	Gomut R.	fer.
Kundal (page 42) -	63	4		
	89	7		
KYRANTY. See Dellamcotta - -	282	5		
LAOUR, in Silhet. See page 42 - -	133	0		
LUCKIPOUR. See Islamabad 1st road - -	77	0		

LURICOOL				
Mulsutgunge, in Mendigunge Road - -	32	1		
Luricool - - -	4	4		
	36	5		
LUSKERPOUR. See Pootya	140	2		
MAHMUDPOUR. See Calcutta - - -	69	5		
MAHABUTPOUR. See Islamabad 2d road -	49	4		
MANICKRAUGE				
Baggrah, in Islamabad 1st road - -	53	6		
Manickrauge - -	7	0	Dackitya N.	fer.
	60	6		
MANGEE				
CHUPRAH - -	482	3		
Gudena - - -	5	2		
Mangee - - -	6	2		
	493	7		
MATCHUACAL. See Naranpour - -	36	5		
MAULDAH, 1st road. See Purneah 1st road.	219	4		
MAULDAH, 2d road by Nattore				
Sibdyhaut - -	8	0	Nullah	ford

(Mauldah 2d road continued)	8	0		
Sampour	6	4	4 Rs & Nullahs	fers.
Sabaar	4	6	Nullah	fer.
Dumroy	6	1	Bunſe R.	fer.
Candapotul	6	1		
Mirzahaut	11	4		
PUCCULOE	6	4		
Attyah	8	2	2 Nullahs	ford
Suntoſh	4	2	Lojung R.	fer.
Gundruckpour	4	7	Joobnee R.	fer.
Belcuchy	9	3	Coni R.	fer.
Dowlatpour	7	1	2 Nullahs 1 fo.	1 fer.
Burrumcopileah	5	6	Foolju R. & 1 N.	fer.
Tarwas	13	6		
Beeas	7	4	Nullah	ford
Cullum	8	1	Goor R.	fer.
Gobinpour	6	5	1 N. & Attri R.	fer.
NATTORE	5	0		
Banchja	5	0	Nullah	ford
Burrumpour	4	3	Barruly R.	fer.
Bowanygunge	9	0		
Simlah	7	4	2 Nullahs	ford
Doolabarry	7	5	Nullah	ford
Chobarya	4	5	Jeel	fer.
Parra	14	6		
Robanpour	8	3		
Iyoe	14	0	Purnabuba & Tangan	fer.
MAULDAH	10	0		
	215	3		
MAULDAH, 3d road by Seerpour. See Patna 3d road	219	0		
MENDIGUNGE				
Futtulah	6	5	2 Nullahs	fer.
Naraingunge	2	6		
	9	3		

(Mendigunge continued)	9	3		
Fringybazar - -	3	1	1 Nullah & Issamutty R	fer.
Surajabads - -	8	4		
Rajabary - -	4	2	Nullah	fer.
Mulsutgunge - -	6	7	Calligonga R.	fer.
Cautekpour - -	6	6		
Boyrah - - -	7	4	2 Nullahs	fer.
Serampour - -	7	4		
Chogong - - -	4	3		
Cusarya - -	4	6	Nullah	fer.
Mendigunge - -	10	0		
	73	0		
MEENKOOT				
Azimgunge, in Benares 1st road - -	144	7		
Goas - -	7	4	Nullah	ford
Chatti - - -	7	0	Ditto	ford
Bogwangola - -	8	4	Culcutty R.	fer.
Meenkoot - - -	8	5		
	176	4		
MIDNAPOUR, 1st road				
CALCUTTA - -	179	5		
MIDNAPOUR (page 45)	74	4		
	254	1		
MIDNAPOUR, 2d road				
Mauncore, in Ganjam Road	214	2		
MIDNAPOUR, as before	42	5		
	256	7		
MIRJANAGORE				
MOORLEY, in Calcutta Road - - -	105	4		
Milladinga - -	5	4		
Momarackpour - -	8	7	Nullah	ford
Mirjanagore - -	6	0		
	125	7		

MIRZAGUNGE				
Backergunge - -	99	4		
* *Mirzagunge* - -	17	0		
	116	4		
MODARGUNGE				
Naranpour, in Bisnee Road	104	1		
Mohungunge - -	4	7		
Golabary - -	9	4	Jenni R.	ford
Modargunge - -	7	0		
	125	4		
MODDIPOUR. See Baminy - -	96	2		
MOMANSING, or Bokinagur. See Susung	90	1		
MONGHIR. See Benares 1st road - -	347	0		
MONGULHAUT. See Buxaduar - -	215	0		
MOODUPOUR, in Pookareah. See Bisnee -	86	5		
MOORLEY, or Jessore. See Calcutta - -	105	4		
MOORSHEDABAD, 1st road. See Benares 1st road - - -	164	7		

MOORSHEDABAD, 2d road by Hajygunge				
Hajygunge, in Calcutta road - - -	40	2		
Kishnapour - -	9	0		
Angordya - -	4	5		
Cameldiggy - -	8	0	Nullah	ford
Bailguchy - -	11	1		
Moddapour (Pangsa) -	7	1	Chundnah	fer.
Soripour - -	8	2		
Comercally - -	4	6		
Custee - - -	10	4		
Damadure - -	11	0		
Hurrysongkor - -	10	4		
Culcully Termony -	11	4	Jellinghee R.	ford
Azimgunge - -	8	2		
Dultabazar - -	11	6		
Balloo - - -	2	5	Nullah	fer.
MOORSHEDABAD (*Mooty-jyl*) - - -	5	5		
	164	7		
MULFUTGUNGE. See Mendigunge -	32	1		
MUSTAN-GUR. See Bux-aduar - -	132	0		
MUTLUPGUNGE. See Islamabad 1st road	40	6		
NABOBGUNGE (Hoodje-rapour). See Purneah 1st road - - -	181	6		

NAGORE, or Birboom. See Benares 2d road - -	235	4		
CHUTA-NAGPOUR. See Doesah - -	440	0		
NARANPOUR Aurung				
Allynyah, in Islamabad 1st road - - -	25	5		
Coweddy - -	9	0	Gomut R.	fer.
Matchuacal - -	2	0		
Naranpour - -	2	5	Nullah	fer.
	39	2		
NARANGUNGE. See Mendigunge - -	9	3		
NARANGUR. See Ganjam	259	5		
NATTORE. See Mauldah 2d road - -	130	1		
NAUTPOUR. See Ammerpour - - -	328	6		
NOGONG				
Seerpour, in Purneah 2d road - - -	110	0		
Singaryah - -	7	2		
Koory - -	8	0		
Champapour - -	6	6	Nagore N.	ford
Belgurrya - -	10	0		
Nogong - -	5	5	Jubuna R.	ford
	147	5		

NOORNAGUR				
Gowrypour, in Kundal Road - - -	31	5		
Salyacondy - -	6	0	Nullah	ford
Tulah - -	9	4	Gomut R.	fer.
Mokimpour - -	7	0	Nullah	ford
Noornagur - -	9	0	Ditto	ford
	63	1		
NOORNAGUR 2d road, by Nurſingdee				
Corallyah, in Azmerigunge Road - - -	35	7		
Ibrampour - -	7	0	Nullah	ford
Budagoſſa - -	4	4	Ditto	ford
Noornagur - -	12	0	Ditto	ford.
	59	3		
NOORPOUR				
Pattergotta - -	6	0	Boorygonga & Dollaſerry Rs	fer.
Solagur - -	7	6		
Rarykal - -	5	4		
Noorpour - -	7	0		
	26	2		
NOWGONG				
Ghyhutta, in Hurryal Road	91	7		
Nowgong - -	7	3		
	99	2		
NOWADAH				
Curree, in Benares 2d road - - -	385	7		
Nowadah - -	9	0		
	394	7		

NUDDEAH				
KISHENAGUR, in Burdwan 2d road - -	140	7		
Nuddeah - - -	9	0	Hoogly R.	fer.
	149	7		
NULDINGAH				
Jennidah, in Burdwan 2d road - -	94	3		
NULDINGAH -	8	6		
	103	1		
NULSHI Imaumpour. See Purneah 2d road -	79	6		
NURILAPOUR. See Calcutta - - -	33	2		
OLYAPOUR. See Bisnee	175	0		
OUDANULLA. See Benares 1st road - -	230	5		
OSUNPOUR. See Susung	62	7		
PACHETE. See Doesah	285	7		
PALAMOW				
Petrabad in Doesah Road	354	7		
* *Goleeah*, or *Golah* -	8	4		
* *RAMGUR* - -	12	0		
PALAMOW (page 53)	124	0		
	499	3		

PARADANGA, in Bittrebund. See Bittrebund	201	2		
PATNA, 1st road by Monghir. See Benares 1st road	446	4		
PATNA, 2d road by Birboom				
Islamnagur, in Benares 2d road	367	3		
PATNA (page 57)	78	0		
	445	3		
PATNA, 3d road by Mauldah				
Eetacola, in Purneah 2d road	146	4		
Jamaulgunge	6	6	Nullah	ford.
Saumgunge	7	6	Ditto	ford
Conchon	12	0	Attri R.	fer.
Seebpour	4	6		
Teelna	4	1		
Nishanpour	6	2		
Hopponyah Gaut	4	0		
Ponkapukre	6	0	Parnabubah R.	fer.
Sawaan	11	0		
MAULDAH	9	7	Tangan R. & 1 N	fer.
Cotwally	2	7	Mahanada R.	fer.
Aamgatch	6	7		
RAJEMAL	10	6	Ganges R.	fer.
PATNA (page 55)	209	3		
	448	7		
PATTERGOTTA, in Attyah				
Tizgong	5	0		
Tunghee Bridge	8	4		
Commarjury	5	2		
	18	6		

(Pattergotta continued) -	18	6		
Caſſimpour - -	4	1	Nullah	fer.
Muddupour (Talipabads)	4	5		
Callyacure - -	6	5		
Curypara - -	1	3		
Pattergotta - -	8	2		
	43	6		
PIALAPOUR				
Callatyah - -	9	4	Boorygonga R.	fer.
Saapour - - -	9	3	{ Dollaterry R. and 1 Nullah }	fer.
Sunegar - - -	5	2	Nullah	fer.
Pialapour - -	7	0		
	31	1		
PLASSEY. See Cutwa	168	1		
POINTY				
Terriagully, in Benares 1ſt road - - -	269	2		
Pointy - - -	8	0		
	277	2		
POOTYA, in Luſkerpour				
NATTORE, in Mauldah road - - -	130	1		
Chandpour - -	5	0		
Pootya - - -	5	1		
	140	2		
POOKARYAH. See Biſnee	86	5		
PUBNA. See Benares 1ſt road - - -	98	7		

PUCCULOE. See Mauldah 2d road - -	49	4		
PUNDUAH				
Agnah, in Silhet Road -	115	4		
Nabobgunge - -	10	6	2 Nullahs	ford
Rufilgunge - -	4	6	Nullah	ford
Digley - - -	9	6	Ditto	fer.
Inchacolus - -	8	6	2 Nullahs	ford
* *Punduah* - -	8	0	Surmah R.	fer.
	157	4		
PURNEAH, 1st road				
Comitpour, in Benares 1st road - - -	105	1		
Burkagaffy - -	5	2		
Battoryah - -	11	0		
Pokaryah - -	8	6		
Hazeryhutty - -	5	5		
Surda - - -	4	0	Nullah	ford
Baulcah - - -	12	2		
Comerpour - -	10	6		
Godlagary - -	10	3		
Nabobgunge - -	8	5		
Chappigunge - -	5	4		
Gomaitahpour - -	8	5	Mahanada R.	fer.
Neemgotchy - -	12	0		
English Bazar - -	8	2		
MAULDAH - -	3	3	Ditto	fer.
PURNEAH (page 60) -	74	5		
	294	1		
PURNEAH 2d road, by Dinagepour				
Suntosh, in Mauldah 2d road - - -	62	0		
Potul - - -	10	6	2 Nullahs	ford
Nulshi-Imaumpour -	7	0	Joobnee R.	fer.
Ruminutgunge - -	6	6	2 Nullahs 1 fer.	1 for.
	86	4		

(Purneah 2d road, continued)	86	4		
Pongaſh - -	4	4	Iſſamutty R.	fer.
Bagah-haut - -	4	6		
Chaterpour Gaut -	7	6	Currattya R.	fer.
Seerpour - - -	6	4		
Garrydaw - -	3	0		
Buggoorah - -	11	0		
Cottal - - -	14	0	Nagore N.	ford
Eetacola - -	8	4		
Appole - - -	9	6		
Baugjenny - -	6	6		
Buxigunge - -	4	0	Jubuna	ford
Burnuggur - -	11	0		
Cheentamaun - -	2	2		
Sumdeah - -	11	0		
DINAGEPORE, or *RA-JEGUNGE* - -	11	5	Attri R. Nullah	fer. ford
Rannygunge - -	5	1	Purnabubah R.	fer.
Singong - -	5	4	3 Nullahs	fords
Saddamol - -	6	5	Tangan R.	ford
Bahmor - - -	10	3	Coolick R.	ford
Bindole - -	6	1		
Taujepour - -	8	4	Nagore R.	ford
Rampour - -	9	5		
Hidgeah - - -	7	4	Sudanny N.	ford
Nabobgunge - -	2	3	Mahanada R.	ford
Durghyagunge -	6	6		
Chickneah - -	7	4	Dubelly R.	
PURNEAH - -	4	4		
	283	3		

RADANAGUR. See Keerpoy - - -	230	3		

RAJABARRY. See Mendigunge - -	25	2		

RAJANAGUR				
Pattergotta - -	6	0	Boorygonga & Dollaterry R.	fer.
Surajady - -	5	0		
Duckinchargong -	4	3		
Dunconya - -	5	7	Nullah	ford
Nunkissergunge -	3	5		
Rajanagur - -	5	4	Calligonga R.	fer.
	30	3		
RAJEMAL 1st road. See Benares 1st road -	237	1		
RAJEMAL 2d road. See Patna 3d road -	239	4		
RAJEGUNGE, or Dinagepour. See Purneah 2d road - - -	202	7		
RAMGUR. See Palamow	375	3		
RANGAMATTY. See Bisnee - -	232	3		
RAYMGUNGE, or Saibgunge. See Dellamcotta - -	244	7		
ROGONAUTPOUR. See Doesah - -	297	2		

ROTASGUR				
Tickarry, in Benares 2d road	451	0		
ROTASGUR (page 62)	71	6		
	522	6		
RUNGPOUR. See Buxuaduar - -	191	5		
RUTTUNGUNGE. See Benares 1st road -	65	7		
RYCOTTY.				
Sutalury, in Baminy Road	95	6		
Iraun - - - -	8	5	2 Nullahs	fers.
Rycotty - - -	9	0	3 Nullahs	fers.
	113	3		
RYNABAD				
Culna (Jessore) -	120	5		
Jerrya - -	10	6		
Rynabad - -	4	2		
	135	5		
SAAPOUR. See Pialapour	18	7		
SAGORDEE. See Azmerigunge 2d road -	48	2		
SANTIPOUR. See Burdwan 2d road - -	155	2		
SANASHYGOTTA				
DINAGEPOUR, in Purneah 2d road -	202	7		
Sanashygotta (page 65)	76	1		
	279	0		

SANASHYGUNGE				
Naranpour, in Bisnee Road	104	1		
Sanashygunge - -	9	0		
	113	1		
SARHAUT. See Benares 2d road - -	275	7		
SASERAM 1st road. See Benares 2d road -	510	4		
SASERAM 2d road, by Patna				
PATNA - - -	446	4		
SASERAM (page 8) -	94	3		
	540	7		
SAIBGUNGE Cantonments. See Dellamcotta	244	7		
SAUGDY				
Mahabutpour, in Islamabad 2d road -	49	4		
Saugdy - - -	5	0	Dackitya N.	fer.
	54	4		
SEERPOUR. See Purneah 2d road - -	110	0		
SEEBGUNGE. See Buxaduar - - -	138	2		
SEETACOON. See Islamabed - - -	126	3		

SERAMPOUR Aurung. See Mendigunge -	53	7		
SERAMPOUR, (Danish Factory)				
Chandernagore - -	168	6		
Ghyretty - - -	4	3		
Serampour - -	4	0		
	177	1		
SERRYLE, or Calligos. See Bangah - -	62	5		
SHAZADPOUR				
Attyah, in Mauldah 2d road	57	6		
Huttybarry - -	10	0	Lojung and Joohnee Rs.	fers.
Bailtoll - - -	7	4	Nullah	fer.
Shazadpour - -	4	0	Coni R.	fer.
	79	2		
SHEERPOUR-Duscownyah				
Sagordee, in Azmerigunge 2d road - -	48	2		
Toke, or Tope - -	4	0	Little Burrampooter & Banar R.	fers.
Bysheeah - - -	5	0		
Sanctura - -	7	6		
Rowah - - -	6	4		
Koryde - - -	3	0		
Callygunge - -	7	3		
Baboocally - -	6	0		
Sowarah - - -	5	1		
Bygonbary - -	7	5	Nullah	ford
Peeärpour - -	9	0		
Rajegunge - -	1	0	Burrampooter R.	fer.
	110	5		

(Sheerpour continued) -	110	5		
Rogonautpour - -	10	0		
Sheerpour - -	7	2		
	127	7		
SHILBERIS, or Buggoorah. See Purneah 2d road -	124	2		
SIBNIBAS. See Burdwan 2d road - -	127	5		
SICLYGULLY. See Benares 1ſt road - -	256	4		
SILHET 1ſt road, by Amerigunge - -				
Azmerigunge - -	102	0		
Banniachung - -	8	1		
SILHET (page 129) -	45	0		
	155	1		
SILHET, 2d road				
Lacki (page 69) -	81	0		
Sujatpour - -	7	6		
Banniachung - -	12	1	Brack R.	fer.
SILHET, as before -	45	0		
	145	7		
SILHET, 3d road by Torroff				
Putyajury, in Bangah Road	105	3		
Dewanbazar - -	12	0	Brack R.	fer.
Soydpour - -	4	4	Nullah	fer.
Aurungpour - -	6	3	2 Nullahs	ford
* Byragvhaut - -	9	6		
* *SILHET* - - -	10	1	Soormah R.	fer.
	148	1		

SOORY, or Hyderabad. See Benares 2d road -	219	4		
SOOTY. See Benares 1st road - - -	200	0		
SUJATPOUR. See Silhet 2d road - -	88	5		
SUNERGONG				
Polatgunge - -	7	6	Dooli N.	fer.
Sunergong - -	5	6	Luckya R.	fer.
	13	4		
SUNERAMPOUR. See Azmerigunge, 1st road	56	1		
SURDA. See Purneah 1st road - -	139	6		
SUSUNG Purgannah				
Sagordee, in Azmerigunge 2d road - -	48	2		
Agarasondu - -	3	0	Burrampooter R.	fer.
Dugdugga - -	8	7		
Osunpour - -	2	6	Nursundy N.	fer.
Sunhatta - -	8	0	Nullah	ford
Modupour - -	5	0		
Moddergunge - -	6	2	Ditto	ford
Bokinagur, or *Momansing*	8	0		
Simulcandy - -	13	2	2 ditto	fer.
Cungas Ferry -	7	3	Cungas R.	fer.
Duregapour Cutcherry	9	3	Nullah	ford
	120	1		

SUTALURY. See Baminy	95	6		
TALIPABADS. See Pattergotta - -	27	4		
TAUJEPOUR. See Purneah 2d road -	245	1		
TEETBADDY Aurung Perralyah, in Azmerigunge 2d road - -	28	2		
Teetbaddy - -	9	4		
	37	6		
TIPERAH, or Commillah. See Kundal - - -	59	2		
TIZGONG - -	5	0		
TORROFF. See Bangah	98	5		
TUNGHY. See Bowall	13	4		

CROSS ROADS

OF

BENGAL AND BAHAR.

CROSS ROADS OF BENGAL AND BAHAR.

BAHAR to *DAÖUDNAGUR*. 86 : 2.

Names of Places.	M.	F.	Rivers and Nullahs	
Suan - - - -	10	4	Banoura	ford
Caramgunge - -	10	4	Nullah	ford
Tillurah - - -	5	4		
Cakow - - -	7	6	Nullah	ford
Jehenabad - -	6	2	Nullah	ford
Noyah - - -	9	6	Nullah	ford
Pondil - - -	8	0	Nullah	ford
Hummidnagore - -	10	0	2 ditto	fors.
Pattypour - - -	11	0	Pompon R.	ford
Daöudnagur - -	7	0		

BAHAR to *DURBUNGAH*. 84.

Names of Places.	M.	F.	Rivers and Nullahs	
Merachuck - -	10	0	Nullah	ford
Bettaw - - -	6	0		
Bar - - - -	8	0	Mahany	ford
Rajowly - - -	5	6	Ganges R.	fer.
Mowah - - -	5	0	Byar N.	fer.
Dulsingerrah - -	7	0		
Pattailly - - -	10	4		
Nagorbussy - - -	7	4	Little Gunduck	ford
Ballypour - -	8	6		
Badapour - - -	8	6	Buckia R.	ford
DURBUNGAH - -	6	6		

BAHAR to *TICKARRY*. 59.

Names of Places.	M.	F.	Rivers and Nullahs	
Janoureah - - -	12	4		
Catowry - - -	6	4	Banoura	ford
Islampour - - -	6	4		
Lucknore - - -	8	4	2 Nullahs	fors.
Pibiggah - - -	14	0	Nullah	ford
Tickarry - - -	11	0	Nullah	ford

BALASORE to *HARRIERPOUR*. 30 : 6

Sageefpatna	5	4	Sone and Gongahar Rs	fers.
Juredar	8	0		
Mauntree	3	0		
Arputter	10	2		
HARRIERPOUR	4	0	Nullah	ford

BAULEAH to *COMERCOLLY*. 58 : 0.

Pokaryah (page 222)	18	3		
Panchefurra Gaut	6	6		
Choculo	2	3	Ganges	fer.
Golebattam	10	0		
Cuftee	10	0		
Comercolly	10	4	Gorroy	ford

BETTYAH to *CHUPRAH*. 85 : 6

Taujepour. (See Buxar to Bettyah)	64	2		
Seray	4	4		
Sumaferay	5	4		
CHUPRAH	11	4		

BETTYAH to *DURBUNGAH*. 106 : 7.

Turki (page 11)	64	3		
Tingrah	4	4		
Chotah	12	0	Buckya R.	ford
Changail	4	0		
Barwarah	10	0		
DURBUNGAH	12	0	Bogmutty	ford

BETTYAH to *SECUNDERPOUR*. 85 : 6.

Semrah. (See Buxar to Bettyah)	34	4		
Butuah	9	2		
Buraryah	5	6	Little Dar R.	ford

BETTYAH to *SECUNDERPOUR*. 85 : 6. (Continued)

Sewan - - -	10	0		
Aundar - - -	9	6	Dar R.	ford
Durowly Gaut - -	13	0	Jerry R.	ford
Secunderpour - -	3	4	Dewa R.	fer.

BISSUNPOUR to *PATCOOM*. 116.

Puruttumpour - -	9	0		
Jambuddeah - -	11	0		
Partchtool - -	4	0		
Manboom (page 39) -	37	1		
Patcoom (page 54) -	54	7		

BISSUNPOUR to *BURRABOOM*. 82 : 7.

Manboom, as above -	61	1		
Mudjehara - - -	10	0		
Muccroo - -	8	0		
Burraboom - - -	3	6		

BISSUNPOUR to *SOORY*. 72 : 7.

Barra - - -	8	0		
Soonamooky - - -	12	0		
Plasdungah - -	6	4		
Nuddyah - - -	9	0	Dummooda	ford
Jamuah - - -	9	2		
Cotah - - -	11	0	Adji R.	ford.
Kissnagur - - -	5	4		
Soory - - -	11	5		

BOGARYAH to *DURRAMPOUR*. 13.

Kissunpour - - -	6	0	Chundun N.	ford
Asnaha - - -	4	6		
Durrampour - -	2	2		

BOGLIPOUR to *BERNAGUR*. 65 : 2.

Seebgunge - - -	6	2	Boglipour N. / Ganges R.	ford / fer.
Allumgunge - - -	9	2		
Bidgee - - -	5	2	Gogary R.	fer.
Bicknee - - -	5	2		
Bowanipour - -	8	0		
Saidgunge - - -	4	0		
Natpour - -	6	2		
Debrah - - -	5	2		
Rupoly - - -	6	6		
Bernagur - - -	9	0		

BOGLIPOUR to *PURSAUMMA*. 81 : 2.

Seebgunge - - -	6	2	Boglipour N. / Ganges R.	ford / fer.
Bepour - - -	5	6		
Jewky - - -	7	0		
Loaky - - -	6	4	Gogary R.	fer.
Baroneah - - -	4	2		
Mynatnagur - - -	11	0		
Simree - - -	13	0		
Bongamah - - -	10	4		
Nohutta - - -	10	6		
Pursaumma - -	6	2		

BURDWAN to *CHANDERNAGORE*. 48 : 4.

First Road.

Purlah - - -	9	2		
Jowgong - - -	12	0		
Malparah - - -	14	4		
Powanan - - -	3	0		
Chandernagore - -	9	6	2 Nullahs	fer.

Second Road. 49 : 1.

Bansberryah (page 15) -	41	4		
HOOGLY - - -	3	2		
Chandernagore - -	4	3		

BURDWAN to *CHINSURAH*. 46 : 4.

HOOGLY (as above) -	44	6		
Chinsurah - - -	1	6		

BURDWAN to *GHYRETTY*, by Deneacolly. 51 : 6.

Bundipour (page 148) -	37	3		
Nallycure - - -	2	6	Nullah	ford
Nuslipour - - -	5	4		
Ghyretty Cantonments -	6	1	Sersetty	ford

BURDWAN to *TAMLOOK*. 79 : 5.

Selimabad (page 148) -	17	1		
Shawabad - - -	11	0	Nullah	ford
Bilegur - - -	5	0		
Kistnagur - - -	10	4		
Omptah - - -	13	0		
Baugnan - - -	9	0	Dummooda R.	fer.
Bynapour - - -	5	0		
Tamlook - - -	9	0	Roopnaran R. and a Nullah.	fers.

BURDWAN to *BUDGEBUDGE*. 72 : 1.

Omptah (as above) -	56	5		
Manickpeer Durga - -	5	6		
Budgebudge - -	9	6	Hoogly R.	fer.

BURDWAN to *NUDDEAH*. 39 : 2.

Sacheroy haut (page 196)	25	0		
Summutgur - -	8	6	Curree R.	fer.
Nuddeah - - -	5	4	Nullah	ford

BURDWAN to *JELLINGHY*. 92 : 2.

Plassey (p. 92.) - - -	47	4		
Ballitungby - -	12	6		
Putkabarry - -	6	4		

BURDWAN to *JELLINGHY*. 92 : 2. (Continued)

Coosubaryah - -	10	4		
Dogassey - - -	3	4		
Culcully River - -	6	6	- -	ford
Jellinghy - - -	4	6		

BURDWAN to *RAJEMAL*. 134 : 6

Assoah (page 90) -	46	1		
Moneegong - -	3	4	More R.	ford
Curgong - - -	6	2		
Seerpour (Jillee) - -	7	2		
Pazgong - - -	5	7	Dwarka R.	ford
Sonkoe - - -	7	4		
Mirzapour - - -	7	5		
Belgotta - - -	4	4	Bansli R.	fer.
Gareeub Field - -	5	2		
Sooty - - -	3	6		
RAJEMAL (p. 37.) - -	37	1		

BURDWAN to *SAINPAHARY*. 42 : 2.

Dignagur (p. 56) - -	20	0		
Balkee - - -	4	2		
Batcoorah - -	5	3		
Comerbazar - -	8	0		
Sainpahary - -	4	5		

BURDWAN to *LACARACOONDAH*. 67 : 1

Okerah (p. 58.) - -	55	1		
Kinnerah - - -	7	0	Adji R.	ford
Lacaracoondah -	5	0		

BURDWAN to *RADNAGUR*. 45 : 4.

Maddapour (p. 103.) -	36	0		
Keerpoy - - -	7	4		
Radnagur - - -	2	0		

BURDWAN to *CHANDERCOONA*.

It lies about five miles to the westward of Jacrah. See p. 103.

BUXAR to *BETTYAH*. 137 : 1.

Gudrajegunge (p. 8.)	38	1		
Luchmonchupra - -	11	0		
Mangee - - -	7	4	Ganges R.	fer.
Jaitpour - - -	5	2		
Taujepour - -	11	0		
Bunsi - - -	8	4	Dar R.	ford
Covaspour - -	5	0		
Sair - - -	9	2		
Semrah - - -	7	0		
Serayah - - -	5	2	Gunduck R.	fer.
Burhurva - - -	6	2		
Sunnoul - - -	3	4		
Jugdispour - -	7	2		
BETTYAH - -	12	2		

BUXAR to *SASERAM*. 52 : 6.

Byree - - -	6	2		
Pursottompour - -	7	0	Torah N.	ford
Dunsway Susoundar -	4	6		
Sigatty - - -	5	0		
Koond - - -	6	2		
Noka - - -	9	4		
Burrong - - -	5	4		
SASERAM - -	8	4		

BUXAR to *ROTAS-GUR*. 87 : 4.

Noka (as above) - -	38	6		
* Sidowly - -	14	4		
* Tiloutta - -	15	0		
Callvampour - -	12	2		
ROTAS-GUR - -	7	0	Nullah	ford

BUXAR to *RAMGUR*. 223.

SASERAM (as above) -	52	6		
Dander - - -	13	0		
Serris - - -	7	2	Soane R.	ford
Norungah - - -	10	6		
Seerpour - - -	12	0		
Beliara - - -	9	2		
Sheergotty - -	12	0	Bura N.	ford
Myapour - - -	4	0		
Luseengnuh - -	12	4	Nullah	ford
Chetrah, or *Chittrah* -	11	4		
Latewah - - -	10	4		
Buggrah - - -	4	6		
RAMGUR (p. 41.) -	60	6		

BUXAR to *KOONDAH*. 148.

Beliara (as above) -	105	0		
* Dumroy - -	10	4		
Eemangunge - -	7	0		
Kooty - - -	7	4		
Jeembaree - -	9	4		
Koondah - -	8	4		

BUXAR to *DÄOUDNAGUR*. 45 : 5.

Dumroy - - -	12	3		
Hochanya - -	7	4		
Nowanagur - -	7	2		
Kytee - - -	11	4		
Daöudnagur - -	7	0	Soane R.	ford

CHITTIGONG (or ISLAMABAD) to *SILHET*. 229 : 7.

Jurilgunge (p. 78.) -	44	6		
Subapour - - -	7	4		
Chuckelkya - -	5	2	Fenny R.	ford
Duspour - - -	7	6		
Kundal - - -	6	0		
Choudagong - -	12	0		
Boggasi - - -	6	2		

CHITTIGONG (or ISLAMABAD) to *SILHET*. 229 : 7.
(Continued)

COMILLAH, or *TIPERAH*	12	3		
Loagur - - -	9	6	Goomty R.	ford
Carraburra - - -	8	0		
Noornagur - - -	5	0		
Singerbill - - -	12	0		
Pattan - - -	4	4		
Serryle - - -	8	2		
Bejurah - - -	8	4		
Chandpour - - -	8	4		
Rajoorah - - -	6	7	2 Nullahs	fors.
Torroff - - -	7	1	2 Ditto	fors.
Putvajury - - -	6	6		
SILHET (page 228) -	42	6		

CHITTIGONG to *AZMERIGUNGE*. 192 : 5.

Chandpour (as above) -	166	5		
Sujatpour - -	10	0	Brack R.	fer.
Beetalung - - -	7	6		
Azmerigunge - -	8	2		

COMILLAH (or TIPERAH) to *CHANDPOUR*. 44 : 5.

Awmtullah - -	4	2		
Rammoan - - -	9	1		
Burkurry - - -	5	3		
Naranpour - - -	10	5	Nullah (at low water)	ford
Mutlupgunge Boalyah -	4	6	Ditto	ford
Chandpour - - -	10	4		

COMILLAH to *JOOGDYAH*. 50 : 6.

Beegypour - - -	6	2		
Dowlatgunge - -	10	4	Dackitya N.	ford
Dattisur - - -	8	0		
Delluah - - -	4	4		
Buxigunge - - -	6	0		
Colinda - - -	7	0		
Joogdyah - -	8	4		

DARRA to *ROTA* Paſs. 28 : 6.

Bowſce - - -	6	3	Chandun	ford
Bogarya - .. -	8	4		
Doudarry - - -	4	3		
Rota Paſs - - -	9	4		

DARRA to *COGEE-Gaut*, or Paſs. 23 : 2.

Doudarry (as above) -	19	2		
Cogee Gaut - -	4	0		

DARRA to *BOGLIPOUR*. 42 : 3.

Bowſee - -	6	3		
Bogaryah - -	8	4	Chandun N.	ford
Chilkore - -	7	6	Ditto twice	fors.
Ruttungunge - -	8	2	Ditto	ford
BOGLIPOUR - -	11	4		

DARRA to *TERRIAGULLY*. 54 : 4.

Corybazar - - -	10	0		
Byſarree - - -	6	6		
Barkoap - - -	6	2		
Duregapour - -	6	0		
Madrapour - -	6	0		
Diggee - - -	10	0		
Terriagully - -	9	4		

DARRA to *COLGONG*. 50.

Madrapour (as above) -	35	0		
Sowlee - - -	7	4		
Colgong - - -	7	4		

DARRA to *PURNEAH*. 94 : 1.

Buddlegunge (page 100)	45	2		
Pointy - - -	9	2		
PURNEAH (page 60) -	39	5		

DARRA to *CURARYAH*. 20 : 4.

Biſſunpour - -	7	0	Cheere N.	ford
Jumnee - - -	8	0		
Curaryah - -	5	4		

DARRA to *SURYAH*. 39 : 6.

Dunwa - -	11	2		
Caukney - -	5	6		
Jeeagur - -	3	4		
Taljarrah - -	9	0		
Mudwun - - -	4	6		
Suryah - -	5	4		

DARRA to *TUREE*. 28 : 4.

Durrampour - -	7	6		
Luchmypour - -	6	2	Chandun N.	ford
Cudhar - -	3	4	Ditto	ford
Joypour - -	3	0	Ditto	ford
Turee - -	8	0		

DARRA to *PALGUNGE*. 83 : 2.

Cudhar (as above) -	17	4		
Chandun N. - -	4	0	- - -	ford
Deogur - -	10	3		
Roonay - -	4	6	Derwa N.	ford
Cokarah - -	9	4		
Rattajore - -	9	4	Patro N.	ford
Chuckerdaw - -	8	0		
Serampour - -	11	0		
Palgunge - - -	8	5	Burracur R.	ford

DARRA to *CHACKI*, by Jumday. 54 : 6.

Beekunpour - -	6	6		
Jumday - -	6	0	Chandun N.	ford
Bundyſeemur - -	12	0		
Chandun - -	7	6	Ditto	ford

DARRA to *CHACKI*, by Jumday. 54 : 6. (Continued)

Silpherry - -	14	0		
Asnah - - -	4	4		
Chacki - - -	3	6		

DINAGEPOUR to *COOS-BEYHAR*. 89 : 0.

Consumagunge (page 26)	22	4		
Cokesabarry - -	6	0		
Amnagur - -	5	0		
Cochimedu - -	5	0		
Calpauny - - -	10	0	2 Nullahs	fors.
BEYHAR (page 141) -	40	4		

DINAGEPOUR to *BYDELL*. 23.

Comergunge - -	9	6	Purnabubah R.	fer.
Bydell - - -	13	2	Tangan R.	ford

DINAGEPOUR to *CHILMARY*. 86.

Sumdeah - -	11	5	Attri R.	fer.
Poolbarry - -	12	3	2 Nullahs	fors.
Pookaryah - -	7	5	Nullah	ford
Titalbarry - -	10	4	Currattya R.	ford
Burradirga - -	7	2		
Rummatpour - -	10	6		
Pansgutchy - -	10	3	Goggot R.	fer.
Barryile - -	7	4	2 Nullahs	fors.
Chilmary - -	8	0	Serri R. Teesta R.	fers.

DINAGEPOUR to *GOBINGUNGE*. 63 : 4.

Poolbarry (as above) -	24	0		
Joypour - -	4	5		
Nabobgunge - -	6	3		
Doudpour - -	3	4	Nullah	ford
Rannygunge - -	10	6		
GORAGOT - - -	5	0		
Gobingunge - -	9	2	Currattyah R.	ford

DINAGEPOUR to *SEEBGUNGE*. 64 : 6.

Sumdeah	11	5	Attri R.	fer.
Cheentamon	11	0		
Burnuggur	2	2		
Buxigunge	11	0		
Durill	8	6	Jubuna	ford
Syritty	4	6		
Burragypara	6	0	Nullah	ford
Kitchuck	6	0		
Seebgunge	3	3	Nullah	ford

DINAGEPOUR to *CURRYDAH*. 27 : 2.

Sidepour	4	0		
Champertully	8	0		
Dumdumma	7	2		
Nobazar	3	2		
Currydah	4	6		

DINAGEPOUR to *BUDDAUL*. 45 : 7.

Sumdeah	11	5	Attri R.	fer.
Odrain	8	4		
Durool	10	2		
Savadgepour	7	4		
Buddaul	8	0		

DINAGEPOUR to *MAHRAJEGUNGE*. 63 : 3.

Rannygunge	5	1	Purnabubah R.	fer.
Singong	5	4	3 Nullahs	fors.
Little Roopgunge	7	3	3 ditto	fors.
Peergunge	7	2	Tangan N.	ford
Suncowr	7	0		
Rabny	2	5		
Sirrypour	10	0	Nagore R.	ford
Ballygurra	10	0		
Mahrajegunge	8	4		

DYNAPOUR to *HILSAH*. 32 : 4.

Fulwary - -	5	6		
Accownah - -	9	6	Pompon R.	ford
Sunbuy - - -	4	0	Nullah	ford
Hilsah - - -	13	0	Mahany R. & a Nullah	fors.

HOOGLY to *BISSUNPOUR*. 81 : 4.

Powanan - -	9	0	2 Nullahs	fers.
Contool - -	6	0		
Deneacolly - -	6	4		
Dugurry - -	5	4	Nullah	ford
Serrykistnapour -	7	6	Dummooda	ford
Lozimpour - -	5	4		
Gopynotpour - -	8	6		
Indos - - -	10	4		
BISSUNPOUR (page 10)	22	0		

HOOGLY to *JELLINGHY*. 102 : 4.

Gosepour - -	8	0	Hoogly R.	fer.
Hell, or Burrye -	5	0		
Jellinghy (page 11) -	89	4		

HOOGLY to *MIDNAPOUR*. 93.

Chandernagore - -	4	3		
Nussipour - -	9	0		
Nallycure - -	5	4	Sersetty N.	ford
Herpaul - -	4	0		
Rajbulhaut - -	9	2		
Chunderbaun - -	7	4	Dummooda	ford
Dewangunge - -	9	2	Dalkisor R.	ford
Maddapour - -	8	0		
MIDNAPOUR (page 103)	36	1		

HOOGLY to *TAMLOOK*. 65 : 7.

Herpaul (as above) -	22	7		
Kistnagur - -	7	0		
Tamlook. (See Burdwan to Tamlook) - -	36	0		

LUCKIPOUR to *COMILLAH*. 48 : 7.

Gopinotpour - -	2	7		
Derramgunge - -	9	2		
Taltally - -	8	1		
Rokundy - -	3	0		
Monohargunge - -	2	0	Dackitya twice	fers.
Dowlatgunge - -	6	7		
Bagmarra - -	7	0		
Beegypour - -	3	4	Ditto	ford
COMILLAH - -	6	2		

LUCKIPOUR to *JOOGDYAH*. 39 : 2.

Mudgypour - -	4	1	Rummatcally	fer.
Bullooah - -	5	1		
Monarhaut - -	5	1	Nullah	fer.
Santasheeta - -	4	5		
Ramsunker - -	5	2	Noacally	fer.
Mirdah haut - -	2	6		
Guyrah - -	8	0		
Joogdyah - -	4	2		

MIDNAPOUR to *CHINSURAH*. 101 : 7.

Nussipour. (See Hoogly to Midnapour) -	88	5		
Ghyretty - -	6	1		
Chandernagore - -	4	3		
Chinsurah - -	2	6		

MIDNAPOUR to *SOORY*. 120 : 4.

Naradowl (page 103) -	22	1		
Chandercona - -	7	0		
Chuttergunge - -	3	2		
Buddumgunge - -	8	2	Selai R.	ford
Cuttoolpour - -	9	0		
Indos - -	10	4	Dalkisor R.	ford
Gogong - -	7	0	Dummooda	ford
Saturyah - -	7	2		
Dignagur - -	9	0		

MIDNAPOUR to *SOORY*. 120 : 4. (Continued)

Ousgong - -	6	2		
Curnagore - -	5	4		
Soory (page 49) -	25	3		

MIDNAPOUR to *RADNAGUR*. 32 : 7.

Jacrah (page 103) -	28	1		
Keerpoy - -	2	6		
Radnagur - -	2	0		

MIDNAPOUR to *GOTTAUL*. 42 : 2.

Paterrah - -	7	0		
Collinagur - -	4	6		
Shawpour - -	6	0	Cassai R.	ford
Goolgong - -	6	0	Ditto	ford
Chitwa - -	7	4		
Gottaul - -	11	0	Ditto & Selai Rs.	fers.

MIDNAPOUR to *TAMLOOK*. 45 : 4.

Paterrah - -	7	0		
Coosseeah - -	7	2	Cassai R.	ford
Debrah - -	3	2		
Rutoleeah - -	8	0		
Purtabpour - -	5	6	Cossar R.	ford
Tooleah - -	5	6		
Gongacally - -	7	2		
Tamlook - -	1	2		

MIDNAPOUR to *INJELLY*. 79 : 5.

Narangur (page 103) -	19	3		
Mackooryah - -	5	6	Cullyaghi R.	fer.
Pataspour - -	10	0		
Cojurdee - -	9	0		
Bazdebpour - -	10	0		
Roypour - - -	7	4		

MIDNAPOUR to *INJELLY*. 79 : 5. (Continued)

Contai	3	4		
Rusoolpour	9	4		
Injelly	5	0	Nullah	fer.

MIDNAPOUR to *NEELGUR*. 93 : 3.

Narangur (page 103)	19	3		
Balasore (page 30)	61	0		
Neelgur	13	0		

MIDNAPOUR to *PACHETE*. 115 : 4.

Roypour (page 168)	46	2		
Jampurrah	4	6	Cassai R.	ford
Mumrah	8	4		
Supour	7	4		
Hatteaputta	7	4		
Connardee	4	4		
Condeacoorah	6	4	Dalkisor R.	ford
Chatna	5	0		
Tilnar	6	4		
PACHETE (page 52)	18	4		

MIDNAPOUR to *TOMAR*. 146 : 2.

Molecah (page 70)	83	2		
Naringa	8	0		
Bankee	5	6		
Bellipahary	4	0		
Tamoicla	7	0		
Ramgur	4	6		
Gungadee	9	0		
Patcoom	9	4	Subunreka	ford
* *Tomar*	15	0		

MONGHIR to *USLAH Gaut*. 40.

CURRUCKPOUR (page 46)	22	4		
Alligunge	10	4		
Uslab Gaut	7	0		

MONGHIR to *ROGONAUTPOUR*. 184.

Deogur (page 46)	-	90	3		
Operbanda (page 147)	-	31	4		
Silgurryah	-	6	3		
Simlahdy	-	7	2		
Gurhea	-	7	0		
Saugurhea	-	5	6	Adji R.	ford
Ayturah	-	11	6		
Dummooda R.	-	7	0	- -	ford
PACHETE	-	8	7		
ROGONAUTPOUR	-	8	1		

MONGHIR to *NOWADAH*. 81 : 4.

Rampour (page 56)	-	25	3		
Cooserah (page 6)	-	28	4		
Cuttree	-	7	0		
Gereek	-	10	0		
Nowadah	-	10	5	Coory N.	ford

MONGHIR to *GOOMAH*. 138 : 7.

CURRUCKPOUR (page 46)	-	22	4	
Milkee	-	5	0	
Calagong	-	10	0	
Dumnah	-	10	0	
Sonah	-	11	0	
Chacki (page 147)	-	16	0	
Curruckdeah (page 121)	-	17	0	
Carabarry	-	9	6	
Doorndah	-	4	6	
Kifmee	-	10	4	
Doomchauns	-	8	0	
Corrummah	-	7	3	
Goomah	-	7	0	

N. B. Goomah Gaut lies about fix miles N. E. from Goomah.

MONGHIR to *NAUTPOUR*. 101 : 6.

Seral (page 176) -	24	0		
Bernagur (page 140) -	50	2		
Puranpour - - -	5	4		
Maubutgunge - -	7	0		
Cutturah - - -	7	0		
Nautpour - - -	8	0		

NAGORE (or BIRBOOM) to *BISSUNPOUR*. 78.

Lacaracoondah - -	10	6		
Okerah - - -	12	0	Adji R.	ford
Serampour - - -	8	4		
Nuddyah - - -	11	2		
BISSUNPOUR. (See Bissunpour to Soory) - -	35	4		

NAGORE to *RAJEMAL*. 111.

Dulebpour Gaut - -	7	5		
Soory - - -	8	3		
Angergurrya - -	6	2	More R.	ford
Pursundpour - -	10	0	Dwarka R.	ford
Bonhaut - - -	8	0		
Nulbatty - - -	10	3	2 Nullahs	fors.
Kanpour - - -	6	7		
Noangong - - -	9	2	Bansli R.	ford
Omrapour - -	7	0		
Purtabgunge - -	6	0		
Downapour - -	5	2		
RAJEMAL (page 55) -	26	0		

NAGORE to *JUMMUCANDY*. 51 : 1.

Soory (as before) -	16	0		
Hautinagur - -	13	1	More R.	ford
Deckabarry - -	6	7		
Cottree Haut - -	5	0		
Moneegong - -	6	1		
Jummucandy - -	4	0	Ditto	ford

NAGORE to *MONGULKOTE*. 57 : 6.

Illambazar (page 147) -	30	6		
Ramnagur - -	5	4		
Soopour - - -	5	4		
Etinda - - -	6	0	Adji R.	ford
Mustella - - -	3	2		
Mongulkote - -	6	6	Nullah	ford

NAGORE to *BUCCLESORE* Hot Wells. 7 : 2.

Titalbund - -	4	0		
Hot Wells - -	3	2		

NAGORE to *DOBA Gaut*. 14 : 2.

Lettabunny Gaut -	5	2		
Baharow - -	3	4	More R.	ford
Doba Gaut - -	5	4		

N. B. By this Pass the *Mahrattas* entered Bengal in 1742.

NARSINGUR to *PACHETE*. 98 : 6.

Chackdaw - -	9	0		
Golawarry - -	7	0		
Biddidee - -	8	0		
Coleapol - - -	5	0		
Boraady - -	8	6		
Dooldarah - -	7	0		
Manboom - -	4	2	Comaree N.	ford
Jettajoory - -	4	3		
Burgong - -	10	2	Cassai R.	ford
Ludoorcah - -	12	0		
Collabunny - -	6	4		
ROGONAUTPOUR -	8	4		
PACHETE - -	8	1		

NARSINGUR to *JANPOUR*. 43 : 6.

Cowkpara - -	7	0		
Betna - - -	6	0		
Churacooty - -	8	2		

NARSINGUR to *JANPOUR*. 43 : 6. (Continued)

Aurung - - -	6	4		
Kerwa - -	6	2		
Janpour - - -	9	6		

NATTORE to *COMERCALLY*. 50 : 5.

Chuppaleah - -	8	1	Narrud R.	fer.
Kalkapour - -	3	4		
Laudannah - -	5	1	Burreyl R. & a Nullah	fers.
Burkagassey - -	10	4		
Comitpour - -	5	2		
Pubna - - -	6	2	Arti R.	fer.
Comercally - -	11	7	Ganges R.	fer.

NULSHI-IMAUMPOUR to *SHAZADPOUR*. 20 : 6.

Belcuchy - - -	6	4	Coni R.	fer.
Cookanny - -	8	6	3 Nullahs	fors.
Shazadpour - -	5	4	2 ditto	fers.

NULSHI to *JAFFIERGUNGE*. 38 : 4.

Attyab (page 154) -	14	6		
Baubunpara - -	8	6	Nullah	ford
Luckidya Gaut -	3	6	Nullah	fer.
Bissempour - -	6	6	Nullah	fer.
Jaffiergunge - -	4	4	Cantabotey R.	fer.

NULSHI to *DEWANGUNGE*. 61 : 3.

Tentalyah - - -	3	6	Coni R.	fer.
Chandgunge - -	8	4	Nullah	fer.
Sersabarry - -	13	6		
Golabarry - -	12	0	Nullah	ford
Duremote - -	13	2	1 ditto	ford
Dewangunge - -	10	1	3 ditto	fors.

PURNEAH to *ALLYGUNGE*. 46 : 2.

Pokareeah (page 141) -	22	6		
Modar - - -	8	2		
Bahdergunge - -	9	6	Conki R.	ford
Allygunge - -	5	4		

PURNEAH to *CAMVELLAW*. 44 : 6.

Jelalgur - - -	11	0		
Arriah - -	6	2		
Abrireab - - -	9	4	Dubelly R.	ford
Fultawary - -	10	0		
Camvellaw - -	8	0		

PURNEAH to *CHURAMOND*. 57 : 1.

Jagrenatpour - -	11	0		
Duncorah - -	8	0		
Byreeah - - -	9	2		
Carial - - -	6	2		
Mondel - -	5	2		
Dummock Nullah -	5	6	- - - -	ford
Saibgunge - -	4	3	Mahanada R.	fer.
Churamond - - -	7	2	Nagore R.	ford

PURNEAH to *DEEMAH Gaut*. 17.

Ecteeapour (page 87) -	13	2	
Deemah Gaut - -	3	6	

RAJEMAL to *PATCHWARRY*. 77 : 4.

Oudanulla - -	6	4		
Furruckabad - -	11	6		
Banniagong - -	3	2		
Paaly - - -	7	4		
Puccoree (Cutcherry of Awmore) - - -	11	4	Cangdon N.	ford
Dunyamara - -	14	0		
Gideeo - - -	10	0		
Tilliapara - -	7	6		
Patchwarry - -	5	2		

RUNGPOUR to *CHELPESH*, or *JELPESH*. 66 : 1.

Guzgotta - - -	7	4		
Avalyah - -	5	4	Teesta N.	ford
Faasey - - -	5	3		
Haatybunder - -	12	4		
Sarraduby - -	6	0		
Cottah - - -	5	4		
Patgong - -	7	6	Durla R.	ford
Seebgunge - -	6	0		
Botehaut - -	7	0		
Jelpesh - - -	3	0	2 Nullahs	ford

RUNGPOUR to *DEWANGUNGE*. 46 : 6.

Little Jaffiergunge -	8	4		
Gungepour - -	5	2	Goggot R.	ford
Jaffiergunge - -	7	3		
Cochimedu - -	6	3		
Banchdaw - -	9	0		
Dewangunge - -	10	2		

RUNGPOUR to *DEWANGUNGE* (in Patladah). 62.

Palasberry (page 126) -	31	3		
Pannyerbarry - -	5	0		
Dewangunge (page 156)	25	5		

RUNGPOUR to *GULMA*. 109 : 3.

Saibgunge (page 204) -	53	2		
Baccally Haut - -	12	5	Goggot R.	ford
Jelpigory - - -	6	7	Teesta R.	fer.
Bahadure - -	5	6		
Sookanee - -	5	3		
Majelly - - -	4	6	Corto R.	ford
Sanashygotta - -	9	4		
Sileegory - - -	6	6		
Gulma Fort - -	4	4		

RUNGPOUR to *CANTALBARRY* (in Bootan). 72 : 6.

Guzgotta - - -	7	4		
Baninagore - -	9	0	Teesta N.	ford
Lolbazar - - -	11	4		
Gopalgunge - -	12	0	3 Nullahs	fors.
Jelemo Haut - -	3	0	Durla R.	ford
Ryechunga - -	14	6	{ Manshi R. 2 Nullahs	fer. fors.
Calcapoura - -	6	0	2 Nullahs	fors.
Cantalbarry - -	9	0	2 ditto	fors.

RUNGPOUR to *CURYGONG*. 25 : 5.

Moddipour Haut -	11	0	Nullah	ford
Chandamarra - -	6	3	Teesta N.	ford
Curygong - - -	8	2		

RUNGPOUR to *JARBARRY*. 47 : 7.

Jaffiergunge in Dewangunge road - - -	21	1		
Burruah - - -	6	0		
Derwanny - -	6	0		
Consumahgunge - -	7	0		
Jarbarry - - -	7	6	Teesta R.	fer.

RUNGPOUR to *JALALGUNGE*. 15 : 6.

Dowtee - - -	5	0		
Mongulcooty - -	8	0		
Jalalgunge - -	2	6		

RUNGPOUR to *BAGGOA Gaut*. 33 : 6.

Oliapour (page 173) -	23	1		
Annitpour - - -	5	3	Nullah	ford
Baggoa - - -	5	2		

N. B. This is the nearest and best place for embarking on the river Burrampooter.

SAIBGUNGE, or RAYMGUNGE, to *JELPESH*. 15 : 6.

Beekrohaut - -	7	4	Jeel	ford
Botehaut - - -	5	2		
Jelpesh - - -	3	0	Durla R.	ford

SAIBGUNGE to *BULRAMPOUR*. 56 : 3.

Bagdogra - - -	8	0		
Patgong - - -	4	0	Durla R.	ford
Balla-haut - -	5	4		
Coosmary-haut -	4	6	Nullah	ford
Botehaut - - -	8	2	5 Nullahs	fors.
BEYHAR - -	11	0	Manshi R.	fer.
Mawamary - -	6	7		
Bulrampour - -	8	0		

SAIBGUNGE to *RANGAMATTY*. 98 : 2.

Chowa-Raja-haut -	9	3		
Cottah - - -	5	0		
Siddelcusy - - -	7	4		
Lolbazar - -	8	5		
Burtar-haut - -	9	6		
Mongul-haut - -	5	4		
Foolbarry Gaut - -	7	0	Durla R.	ford
Coorsah - - -	2	6	Neelcomer R.	fer.
Boot-haut - -	6	0		
Rottinpour - -	7	2		
Contaljalla - -	6	4		
Binnaserra - -	3	4	Sunecos R.	fer.
Terria - - -	7	0		
Mettabaug - -	6	4		
RANGAMATTY -	6	0	Gaddada R. Sunecos R.	fers.

SAIBGUNGE to *CHICHACOTTA*. 53 : 2.

Balla-haut (as above) -	17	4		
Neetanundy - -	7	4		
Ryechunga - - -	8	6	Manshi R.	ford
Dahogurry - -	11	0	Toresha R.	fer.
Chichacotta - -	8	4	Surradinga R.	fer.

SAIBGUNGE to *TAUJEPOUR*. 71 : 6.

Dewangunge	11	6		
Teesta River	4	0	- - -	fer.
Gurriah	12	0		
Gubinagur	9	6	Tangan R.	ford
Seebgunge	4	6		
Jungar	7	2		
Rahny	7	0		
Deergunge	8	6		
Taujepour	6	4		

SERAMPOUR (in Bahar) to *CHACKI*. 35 : 3.

Chuckerdaw	11	0		
Patro Nullah	9	0	- -	ford
Doolumpour	4	3		
Chacki	11	0	Adji R.	ford

SERAMPOUR to *COORUNG*. 30.

Hylapour	11	4		
Rajabeta	8	4		
Coorung	10	0		

SERAMPOUR to *AYTURAH*, by the Northern Road. 55 : 11

Deopour	11	2	Usree N.	ford
Digarry	7	0		
Koortah	6	0		
Fooljury	8	1		
Koolbarya	10	6		
Ayturah	12	0		

SERAMPOUR to *GOOMAH*. 70 : 4.

Palmow	9	0		
Laidah	7	0		
Burkutta	8	0		
Kurkurry	4	4		

SERAMPOUR to *GOOMAH*. 70 : 4. (Continued)

Burmee	3	0		
Markutchoe	8	4		
Jaynagur	13	4		
Goomah	10	6		
Coomah Gaut	6	2		

SILHET to *LAÖUR*. 71 : 4.

Sawgunge	3	4	Soormah R.	fer.
Digley	10	0	Bussya N.	ford
Iuchacolus	8	6	Nullah	ford
Pannyle	10	0	Ditto	ford
Itchamutty Tannah	5	6	Ditto	ford
Solagur	9	0		
Amdabads	9	0	Soormah R.	fer.
Loarchura	8	2		
Laöur	7	2	Rucktee R.	fer.

SULTANGUNGE to *GOGARY*. 18 : 4.

Dumarya	2	0	Ganges R.	fer.
Modypour	8	0		
Gogary	8	4		

BOGARYAH to *LUCHMYPOUR*. 17 : 6.

Jumday	10	2		
Luchmypour	7	4		

BURHAMPOUR to *BALLOO*. 8.
(In Dacca Road.)

Chunacolly	4	0		
Balloo	4	0		

SAIBGUNGE to *CURYGONG*. 67.

Mongulbaut (page 257)	45	6		
Quoilagaut	6	4		
Ponga	5	6		
Curygong	9	0		

BURHAMPOUR to *TITALYAH.* 15 : 4.
(In Rungpour Road)

Chunacolly - - -	4	0	Nullah	fer.
Boyrupour - -	4	4		
Titalyah - - -	7	0		

BURHAMPOUR to *LOWDAH.* 7 : 4.
(In Ballitunghy Road)

Soondipour - -	5	0	
Lowdah - - -	2	4	

BURHAMPOUR to *CALLYONGUNGE.* 13 : 2.
(In Birboom Road)

Moketerpour Chokey -	4	4	Coſſimbuzar R.	ford
Callyongunge - -	8	6	Nullah	ford

BURHAMPOUR to *TERETCOONA.* 10.
(In Birkooty Road)

Coſebaug - - -	5	0	Coſſimbuzar R.	fer.
Teretcoona - -	5	0		

BURHAMPOUR to *MORADBAUG.* 9.

Coſebaug - - -	5	0	Coſſimbuzar R.	fer.
Moradbaug - -	4	0		

SERAMPOUR (in Bahar) to *SARHAUT.* 43.

Baildee - - -	8	4		
Bunſeemy - - -	6	0		
Murgoomora - -	6	4		
Digbad - - -	6	0		
Gunjibady - -	6	0		
Patro Nullah - -	6	0	- - -	ford
Sarhaut - - -	4	0		

AN

INDEX

TO THE

CROSS ROADS, &c.

I N D E X

TO THE

C R O S S R O A D S.

BOGLIPOUR to		Page
Bahar.	*Rampour* -	56
	Bahar -	6
Benares.	*By Patna*	——
Bernagur	*in Purneah*	236
Bettyah.	*By Patna*	——
(another road by Monghir)		
Birboom.	See Nagore	—
Bowanipour	——	236
Bogaryah	——	242
Burdwan.	*Deogur*. See below	——
	Burdwan -	57
Buxar.	*By Patna*	——
Calcutta	——	146,92
Caragola.	*Colgong* -	146
	Caragola -	140
Champernagur.	——	56
Chacki.	*Deogur*. See below	——
	Chacki -	57
Another road.		
	Jumday. See below	——
	Chacki -	243
Chilkore	——	13
Chandun.	*Jumday*. See below	——
	Chandun -	243
Chittigong.	*By Dacca*	——
Colgong	——	146
Cossimbuzar	——	146,92
Cudhar.	*Chilkore* -	13
	Cudhar -	46
Curruckdea.	*Chacki*. See above	——
	Curruckdea	121
Curruckpour	*Ruttungunge*	13
	Curruckpour	22
Dacca.	*By Moorshedabad*	
Darra	——	242
Deogur.	*Chilkore* -	13
	Deogur -	46
Dinagepour.	*Rajemal* -	146
	Mauldah	142
	Dinagepour	156

BOGLIPOUR to		Page
Durbungah.	*Monghir*	56
	Barriapour	10
	Durbungah	66
Durrampour	*Begarya* -	242
	Durrampour	235
Gogary.	*Sultangunge*	56
	Gogary -	259
Goomah.	*Chacki*. See above	——
	Goomah -	250
Guidore.	*Curruckpour*. See above	——
	Mellypour	153
	Guidore -	149
Jauldoe.	*Serampour*. See below	——
	Jauldoe -	182
Islamabad.	*By Dacca*	——
Jumday.	*Chilkore* -	13
	Jumday -	46
Kindooah.	*Darra* -	242
	Kindooah -	156
Luchmipour	*Durrampour*. See above	——
	Luchmipour	243
Madrapour.	*Colgong* -	146
	Madrapour	242
Mauldah.	*Rajemal* -	146
	Mauldah	142
Monghir	——	56
Moorshedabad	——	146
Nagore.	*Deogur*. See above	——
	Nagore -	147
Nautpour.	*Bernagur*	236
	Nautpour	251
Noony.	*Darra* -	242
	Noony -	156
Pachete.	*Deogur*. See above	——
	Pachete -	250
Palgunge.	*Deogur*. See above	——
	Palgunge	243
Patchwarry.	*Darra* -	242
	Patchwarry	142

N. B. Each of the above places is ſituated on a different road leading from Moorſhedabad; and in that part of it where the correſponding road from Burhampour falls in; ſo that by the help of this Index, the Moorſhedabad Tables will alſo ſerve for Burhampour.

COMILLAH, or TIPERAH, to		
Azmerigunge	——	241
Chandpour	——	241
Chittigong	——	241,240
Colinda	——	241
Dacca	——	96
Joogdya	——	241
Luckipour	——	247
Silhet	——	241
Singerbill	——	241
Sujatpour	——	241
Torroff	——	241

DARRA to		
Bahar.	*Chacki* -	243
	Bahar -	57
Barkope	——	242
Birkooty	——	142
Biſſunpour.	*By Nagore*	——
Bogaryah	——	242
Boglipour	——	242
Burdwan.	*By Nagore*	——
Buxar.	*By Patna*	——
Calcutta	——	25
Caragola.	*Buddlegunge*	100
	Pointy -	242
	Caragola -	60
Chacki	——	243
2d road.	*Deogur* -	243
	Chacki -	57
Chittigong	*By Moorſhedabad*	
Chilkore	——	242
Cogee Gaut	——	242
Colgong	——	242
Corybazar	——	242
Cudhar	——	25
Curruckdeah	*Chacki* -	243
	Curruckdeah	121
Curruckpour	*Tarrapour*	116
	Curruckpour	22
Deogur	——	243
Deopour.	*Serampour*	243
	Deopour -	156
Dobogaut	——	156
Durrampour	——	243
Goomah.	*Chacki* -	243
	Goomah -	250
Guidore.	*Chacki* -	243
	Guidore -	57

DARRA to		Page
Jauldoe.	*Palgunge* -	243
	Jauldoe -	182
Jumday	——	243
Jumnee	——	243
Kindoah	——	156
Luchmipour	——	243
Madrapour	——	242
Mobog Gaut	——	25
Monghir	——	116
Moorthedabad	——	100
Nagore, or Birboom	——	25
Noony	——	156
Pachete.	*Deogur* -	243
	Pachete -	250
Palgunge	——	243
Patchwarry	——	142
Patna.	*By Monghir*	
Pointy	——	242
Purneah	——	242
Rajemal.	*Pialpour* -	100
	Rajemal -	246
Ramgur.	*Chacki* -	243
	Goomah -	250
	Ramgur -	177
Roonay	——	243
Rota Paſs	——	242
Sarhaut	——	25
Siclygully.	*Pialapour*	100
	Siclygully -	146
Serampour	——	243
Soory.	*By Nagore*	——
Suryah	——	243
Taljarra	——	243
Tarrapour	——	116
Terriagully	*Pialapour*	100
	Terriagully	146
2d road by Madrapour		242
Turee	——	243

DINAGEPOUR to		
Appole	——	223
Attyah	*Suntoſh*	223,224
	Attyah -	154
Bauleah	*Nobutta* -	102
	Bauleah -	64
Beyhar	——	244

DINAGEPOUR to		Page
Shilberis (or Buggura)		223
Silhet.	*Seebgunge*	245
	Silhet -	181
Taujepour	——	223
DYNAPOUR to		
Fulwarry	——	246
Hilſah	——	246
N. B. All the other great roads to and from Dynapour lead through Patna.		
HOOGLY to		
Benares	*By Burdwan*	
	By Moorſhedabad	
Biſſunpour	——	246
Burdwan	——	236
Calcutta	——	92
Chandernagore	——	92
Chinſura	——	95
Coſſimbazar	——	54
Dacca	——	208
Dinagepour	*By Moorſhedabad*	
Ghyretty	——	92
Jellinghy	——	246
Jeſſore	*Moſundah*	208
	Mullickpour	199
	Dacca -	23
Indos	——	246
Kiſhenagur	*Hell* - -	246
	Kiſhenagur	11
Mauldah.	*By Moorſhedabad*	
Midnapour	——	246
Monghir	——	54,56
Moorſhedabad	——	54,55
Nagore.	*By Burdwan*	
Patna	——	54
2d road by Burdwan		——
Purneah.	*By Moorſhedabad*	
Rajemal	——	54
Rungpour.	*By Moorſhedabad*	
Tamlook	——	246
LUCKIPOUR to		
Bullooah	——	247
Calcutta	*Jaynagur* -	37
	Calcutta -	24

LUCKIPOUR to		Page
2d road by Dacca	-	——
Chandpour	——	37
Chittigong	——	37
Colinda	——	37
Comillah	——	247
Dacca	——	211,210
Joogdyah	——	247
Moorſhedabad	——	111
2d road by Dacca	-	——
Patna.	*By Dacca*	——
Rajabarry	——	37
Silhet.	*By Comillah*	——
MAULDAH to		
Bauleah	——	222
Benares.	*By Patna*	——
Calcutta.	*By Moorſhedabad*	
Dacca	——	213
Dinagepour	——	156
Malduar.	*Meerjaſerra*	44
	Rahny, or Malduar -	61
Moorſhedabad	——	60,26
Nabobgunge	*Chappigunge*	60
	Nabobgunge	26
Patna.	*Rajemal* -	142
	Patna -	55
Purneah	——	60
Rajemal	——	142
Rungpour	——	142
2d road by Dinagepour		——
Seebgunge.	*Niſhanpour*	142
	Ectacola -	154
	Seebgunge	181
Sultanpour.	*Purruah* -	44
	Sultanpour	131
MIDNAPOUR to		
Aminagur	——	168
Ayturah.	*Pachete* -	158
	Ayturah -	90
Bahar.	*By Nagore*	——
Balaſore	——	158,30
Baumeen Paſs	——	70,71
Beercool.	*Narangur*	103
	Beercool -	86
Biſſunpour	——	158

MIDNAPOUR to		Page
Serampour 1st road.	*DebbeYanna*	158
	Serampour	58
2d road.	*Joypour* -	168
	Serampour	182
Sillee.	*Joypour* -	168
	Sillee - -	40
Singboom	——	70,71
Soojanhy Pass	——	71
Soory	——	248
Tamlook	——	248
Tomar	——	249
MONGHIR to		
Ayturah	——	250
Bahar.	*Rampour* -	56
	Bahar -	6
Belliah	——	10
Benares.	*By Patna* ——	
Bettyah	(2 roads)	10
Bernagur	(in Purneah)	
	Seral - -	176
	Bernagur -	140
Beyhar	*Colgong* -	146
	Beyhar -	140
Bissunpour	*By Nagore* ——	
Bogaryah	——	141
Boghpour	——	146
Burdwan.	*By Nagore* ——	
Buxar.	*By Patna* ——	
Calcutta	——	146,92
Caragola.	*Colgong* -	146
	Caragola -	140
Chacki	——	250
Champernagur	——	146
Chilkore	——	141
Chittigong.	*By Dacca* ——	
Cossimbazar	——	146,92
Cooserah	*Rampour* -	56
	Cooserah -	6
Curruckdea	——	250
Curruckpour	——	46
Dacca 1st road	*By Moorshedabad*	
2d road	*By Mauldah*	
Darra	——	141
Deogur	(2 roads)	46,47

MONGHIR to		Page
Dinagepour.	*Rajemal* -	146
	Mauldah -	142
	Dinagepour	156
Dobagaut.	*Darra* -	141
	Dobagaut -	156
Doesah (or Chuta-Nagpour)	*Serampour*. See below	
	Naranpour	182
	Petrabad -	41
	Doesah -	16
Daöudnagur	*By Bahar* ——	
Durbungah.	*Burriapour*	10
	Durbungah	66
Gayah.	*By Bahar* ——	
Gogary	——	176
Goomah	——	250
Guidore.	*Rampour* -	56
	Guidore -	149
Hajypour.	*By Patna* ——	
Jauldoe.	*By Serampour*	
Koondah.	*By Bahar* ——	
Luchmypour	*Bogaryah*	141
	Luchmypour	259
Mauldah	*Rajemal* -	146
	Mauldah -	142
Maissey	——	10,11
Mellypour	*Rampour* -	56
	Mellypour	149
Midnapour	*By Nagore* ——	
Moorshedabad	——	146
Nagore.	*Deogur*	46,47
	Nagore -	147
Nagorbussy	——	10
Nautpour	——	251
Noony.	*Darra* -	141
	Noony -	156
Nowadah	——	250
Pachete	——	250
Palamow.	*Koondah*, as above ——	
	Palamow	174
Palgunge.	*By Serampour*	
Patchwarry	——	141
Patna	——	56
Pointy.	*Colgong* -	146
	Pointy -	140

NAGORE to		Page
Lacaracoonda	——	251
Luchmipour	*Deogur* -	57
	Cudhar -	46
	Luchmipour	25
Manboom	*Lacaracoonda*	251
	Manboom	130
Midnapour.	*By Bissunpour*	
Mobagaut	——	25
Monghir. 1st & best road	*Deogur* -	57
	Monghir	46
2d road, by Rota Pass.	*Deogur* -	57
	Monghir	47
Mongulcote	——	252
Moorshedabad	——	169
Narangur	*By Midnapour*	
Noony	——	25
Omdarra.	*Soory* -	169
	Omdarra -	165
Pachete.	*Lacaracoonda*	251
	Pachete -	90
Palgunge.	*Serampour.* See below	——
	Palgunge	182
Patchwarry.	*Nulhatty* -	251
	Patchwarry	54
Patcoom.	*Lacaracoonda*	251
	Patcoom -	130
Patna	——	57
Rajemal	——	251
Ramgur.	*Lacaracoonda*	251
	Petrabad -	90
	Ramgur -	112
Rogonautpour	*Lacaracoonda*	251
	Rogonautpour	90
Saibgunge.	*By Moorshedabad*	
Sarhaut	——	57
Serampour.	*Ayturah.* See above	——
	Serampour	58
Sillee.	*Rogonautpour.* See above	
	Sillee -	111
Sunamooky	*Nuddyah* -	251
	Sunamooky	235
Tarrapour.	*Deogur* -	57
	Tarrapour -	46

NAGORE to		Page
Turee.	*Sarhaut* -	57
	Turee -	77

NARSINGUR to		
Coleapol	——	252
Huldipookre	——	70
Janpour	——	252
Manboom	——	252
Midnapour	——	70
Pachete	——	252
Rogonautpour	——	252

NULSHI-IMAUMPOUR to		
Attyah	——	122
Belcuchy	——	253
Buggurah (or Shilberis)		222
Bygonbarry.	*Moodupour*	115
	Bygonbarry	75
Dacca	——	154
Dewangunge	——	253
Dinagepour	——	222
Golabarry	——	253
Goragot	*By Seebgunge*	
Jassiergunge	——	253
Moodupour (Pookareeah)		115
Moorshedabad	*Nattore.* See below	——
	Bauleah -	101
	Moorshedabad	64,63
Nattore.	*Cullum* -	122
	Nattore -	27
Rungpour.	*Buggurah*	222
	Rungpour	197
Seebgunge.	*Buggurah*	222
	Seebgunge	197
Seerpour	——	222
Shazadpour	——	253

PURNEAH to		
Allygunge	——	254
Ammerpour	——	1
Benares.	*By Monghir*	——
Bernagur	——	87
Bettyah.	*Durbungah*	176
	Bettyah -	234
Beyhar	——	141

TABLE

OF THE

SUN's RISING AND SETTING.

⁂ The Uſe of the within Table is too obvious to require an explanation. The Latitude of the Place muſt be found in the Map oppoſite to the Title Page. Obſerve, that by Reaſon of the Refraction, the Sun appears to be much higher than it really is; ſo that if the riſing and ſetting be reckoned from the Time when the Body of Sun is quite above the Horizon, it will be neareſt the Truth.

TABLE OF THE SUN's RI

Between the Parallels of

SUN RISES

Month	Day	Day	Month	21° 30′	22° 30′	23°	24°	25°	25° 3
				DEGREES OF					
				h. m.	h. m.	h. m.	h. m.	h. m.	h. m
	—	21	Dec.	6 . 39	6 . 41	6 . 42	6 . 44	6 . 47	6 . 4
Jan.	1	10		6 . 38	6 . 40	6 . 41	6 . 43	6 . 46	6 . 4
	9	2		6 . 36	6 . 38	6 . 39	6 . 41	6 . 43	6 . 4
	15	26	Nov.	6 . 35	6 . 36	6 . 37	6 . 39	6 . 41	6 . 4
	20	21		6 . 33	6 . 35	6 . 36	6 . 37	6 . 39	6 . 4
	25	16		6 . 31	6 . 33	6 . 34	6 . 35	6 . 37	6 . 3
Feb.	1	9		6 . 28	6 . 29	6 . 30	6 . 31	6 . 33	6 . 3
	8	3		6 . 25	6 . 26	6 . 26	6 . 27	6 . 29	6 . 3
	14	27	Oct.	6 . 21	6 . 22	6 . 23	6 . 24	6 . 25	6 . 2
	18	23		6 . 18	6 . 19	6 . 20	6 . 21	6 . 22	6 . 2
	22	19		6 . 16	6 . 17	6 . 17	6 . 18	6 . 19	6 . 2
	26	15		6 . 13	6 . 14	6 . 14	6 . 15	6 . 16	6 . 1
Mar.	2	11		6 . 11	6 . 12	6 . 12	6 . 13	6 . 13	6 . 1
	6	7		6 . 9	6 . 9	6 . 9	6 . 10	6 . 10	6 . 1
	10	3		6 . 6	6 . 7	6 . 7	6 . 7	6 . 7	6 .
	15	28	Sep.	6 . 3	6 . 3	6 . 3	6 . 3	6 . 4	6 .
	20	22		6 . 0	6 . 0	6 . 0	6 . 0	6 . 0	6 .
	25	17		5 . 57	5 . 57	5 . 57	5 . 57	5 . 56	5 . 5
	30	12		5 . 54	5 . 53	5 . 53	5 . 53	5 . 53	5 . 5
Apr.	3	8		5 . 51	5 . 51	5 . 51	5 . 50	5 . 50	5 . 4
	7	4		5 . 49	5 . 48	5 . 48	5 . 47	5 . 47	5 . 4
	11	31	Aug.	5 . 47	5 . 46	5 . 46	5 . 45	5 . 44	5 . 4
	15	27		5 . 44	5 . 43	5 . 43	5 . 42	5 . 41	5 . 4
	20	23		5 . 42	5 . 41	5 . 40	5 . 39	5 . 38	5 . 3
	24	18		5 . 39	5 . 38	5 . 37	5 . 36	5 . 35	5 . 3
May	1	12		5 . 35	5 . 34	5 . 34	5 . 33	5 . 31	5 . 3
	8	5		5 . 32	5 . 31	5 . 30	5 . 29	5 . 27	5 . 2
	15	28	July	5 . 29	5 . 27	5 . 26	5 . 25	5 . 23	5 . 2
	20	23		5 . 27	5 . 25	5 . 24	5 . 23	5 . 21	5 . 2
	25	18		5 . 25	5 . 24	5 . 23	5 . 21	5 . 19	5 . 1
	31	12		5 . 24	5 . 22	5 . 21	5 . 19	5 . 17	5 . 1
June	10	2		5 . 22	5 . 20	5 . 19	5 . 17	5 . 15	5 . 1
	21	—		5 . 21	5 . 19	5 . 18	5 . 16	5 . 13	5 . 1

RISING AND SETTING,

ɛls of 21° 30′ and 30° North.

OF LATITUDE.

	25° 30′	26°	27°	28°	28° 30′	30°				
m.	h. m.	h. m.	h. m.	h. m.	h. m.	h. m.				
47	6 . 48	6 . 49	6 . 51	6 . 53	6 . 54	6 . 58		—	21	June
46	6 . 47	6 . 48	6 . 50	6 . 52	6 . 53	6 . 57		2	10	
43	6 . 44	6 . 45	6 . 48	6 . 50	6 . 51	6 . 54		12	31	
41	6 . 42	6 . 43	6 . 45	6 . 47	6 . 48	6 . 51	July	18	25	
39	6 . 40	6 . 41	6 . 43	6 . 45	6 . 46	6 . 48		23	20	
37	6 . 38	6 . 39	6 . 40	6 . 42	6 . 43	6 . 46		28	15	May
33	6 . 34	6 . 35	6 . 36	6 . 37	6 . 38	6 . 41		5	8	
29	6 . 30	6 . 30	6 . 31	6 . 33	6 . 34	6 . 36		12	1	
25	6 . 26	6 . 26	6 . 27	6 . 28	6 . 29	6 . 31	Aug.	18	24	
22	6 . 23	6 . 23	6 . 24	6 . 25	6 . 26	6 . 27		23	20	
19	6 . 20	6 . 20	6 . 21	6 . 22	6 . 23	6 . 23		27	15	
16	6 . 17	6 . 17	6 . 18	6 . 18	6 . 19	6 . 20		31	11	Apr.
13	6 . 14	6 . 14	6 . 14	6 . 15	6 . 16	6 . 16		4	7	
10	6 . 11	6 . 11	6 . 11	6 . 12	6 . 12	6 . 13		8	3	
7	6 . 7	6 . 8	6 . 8	6 . 9	6 . 9	6 . 9		12	30	
4	6 . 4	6 . 4	6 . 4	6 . 4	6 . 4	6 . 5	Sep.	17	25	
0	6 . 0	6 . 0	6 . 0	6 . 0	6 . 0	6 . 0		22	20	
56	5 . 56	5 . 56	5 . 56	5 . 56	5 . 56	5 . 55		28	15	Mar.
53	5 . 53	5 . 52	5 . 52	5 . 51	5 . 51	5 . 51		3	10	
50	5 . 49	5 . 49	5 . 49	5 . 48	5 . 48	5 . 47		7	6	
47	5 . 46	5 . 46	5 . 46	5 . 45	5 . 44	5 . 44		11	2	
44	5 . 43	5 . 43	5 . 42	5 . 42	5 . 41	5 . 40	Oct.	15	26	
41	5 . 40	5 . 40	5 . 39	5 . 38	5 . 37	5 . 37		19	22	
38	5 . 37	5 . 37	5 . 36	5 . 35	5 . 34	5 . 33		23	18	Feb.
35	5 . 34	5 . 34	5 . 33	5 . 32	5 . 31	5 . 29		27	14	
1	5 . 30	5 . 30	5 . 29	5 . 27	5 . 26	5 . 24		3	3	
7	5 . 26	5 . 25	5 . 24	5 . 23	5 . 22	5 . 19		9	1	
3	5 . 22	5 . 21	5 . 20	5 . 18	5 . 17	5 . 16	Nov.	16	25	
1	5 . 20	5 . 19	5 . 17	5 . 15	5 . 14	5 . 12		21	20	
9	5 . 18	5 . 17	5 . 15	5 . 13	5 . 12	5 . 9		26	15	Jan.
7	5 . 16	5 . 15	5 . 12	5 . 10	5 . 9	5 . 6		2	9	
5	5 . 13	5 . 12	5 . 10	5 . 8	5 . 7	5 . 3	Dec.	10	1	
3	5 . 12	5 . 11	5 . 9	5 . 7	5 . 6	5 . 2		21	—	

SUN SETS